The Play of the Personal

Complicated Conversation

A Book Series of Curriculum Studies

William F. Pinar
General Editor

Vol. 3

PETER LANG
New York • Washington, D.C./Baltimore • Bern
Frankfurt am Main • Berlin • Brussels • Vienna • Oxford

Alice J. Pitt

The Play of the Personal

Psychoanalytic Narratives of Feminist Education

PETER LANG
New York • Washington, D.C./Baltimore • Bern
Frankfurt am Main • Berlin • Brussels • Vienna • Oxford

Library of Congress Cataloging-in-Publication Data

Pitt, Alice J.
The play of the personal: psychoanalytic narratives
of feminist education / Alice J. Pitt.
p. cm. — (Complicated conversation; vol. 3)
Includes bibliographical references (p.) and index.
1. Feminism and education. 2. Psychoanalysis and education.
3. Teacher-student relationships. 4. Narration (Rhetoric)—
Psychological aspects. I. Title. II. Series.
LC197 .P58 370'.82—dc21 2002013060
ISBN 0-8204-6300-0
ISSN 1534-2816

Die Deutsche Bibliothek-CIP-Einheitsaufnahme

Pitt, Alice J.:
The play of the personal: psychoanalytic narratives
of feminist education / Alice J. Pitt.
–New York; Washington, D.C./Baltimore; Bern;
Frankfurt am Main; Berlin; Brussels; Vienna; Oxford: Lang.
(Complicated conversation; Vol. 3)
ISBN 0-8204-6300-0

Cover design by Dutton & Sherman Design

275 Seventh Avenue, 28th Floor, New York, NY 10001
www.peterlangusa.com

Contents

Preface: William F. Pinar

The Time of Self-Difference and Self-Resistance

The time of *Nachträglichkeit*, then, is the time of self-difference and self-resistance.
—Alice J. Pitt

"What do we use the personal to do?" Alice Pitt asks. One use is narrative, she answers; we employ stories that are our own in order "to make good our lives." Stories enable us to make sense of ourselves, so that our lives become meaningful. In doing so, we are performing more than a literary operation. "We might," Pitt suggests, "understand our interpretative narratives as psychic events" (69). They are about "the world," but, as we learn in this profoundly provocative book, they are about ourselves as well.

A second use of the personal occurs, Pitt points out, when we—teachers and students—face demands that we include the details of our private lives as curriculum content. While personal stories can help us to forge relationships with others, Pitt allows, the demand that we "share" can sometimes "feel creepy." Why? If Winnicott's postulation of a "secret self" has merit (as Pitt implies it does), it can be ontologically awkward to be faced with a pedagogical demand to disclose ourselves. Such a demand can feel like a violation. Given the hide-and-seek character of communication, we cannot be surprised, as Pitt so nicely puts it, that "ambivalence marks the use of the personal itself" (90)

The Secret Self

Near the end of his life, Pitt tells us, D. W. Winnicott explored "the right not to communicate," a right tantamount to "a protest from the core of me to the frightening fantasy of being infinitely exploited" (see 85). Winnicott associated this "frightening fantasy" with dependence in two orders of relationships: mother/child and analyst/analysand. We might add a third: teacher/student.

Not unlike the phenomenologist Langeveld's (1983a, 1983b) notion of the "secret place," Winnicott postulated, at the individual's very core, the existence of a separate and secret self. The existence of such a "self," Pitt suggests, "opens the underside of object-relations theory" (85). While acknowledging the social and specifically collaborative character of self-formation, the "secret" self signals "a protest" to the pleasures of communication. Our profound need to communicate and our need to use the communications of others to constitute individuality are mediated by an equally pressing need to defend against intrusion into the sphere of our most inner and secret selves. Consequently, Pitt concludes, "communication itself is experienced as an urgent game of hide and seek" (85). Moreover, she continues, the idea that communication with the secret self is experienced as profoundly exploitative poses new challenges to psychoanalysts for whom the analysand's refusal of analytic interpretations continues to be construed primarily as resistance to be worked through. It is also a challenge to educators who value the personal as the grounds of teaching and learning (85).

Winnicott's metaphoric use of the popular children's game of "hide-and-seek" underscores, Pitt suggests, the ambivalent labor of communication, including its corresponding states of illusion and disillusionment. "Our capacity to think begins with our tolerance of disillusionment," Pitt asserts (93). The three moments of the personal that so preoccupied Winnicott—illusionment, disillusion, and re-illusionment—caution, Pitt counsels, against demanding too much of the personal.

Pitt is surely right when she asserts that "the personal is something a great deal more complicated than either the developers of the French lesson or some educational researchers might be willing to admit" (91). She elaborates:

> The personal is not merely a set of attributes that can be pointed to or named, nor is it a bank of experiences to be drawn upon unproblematically to render the world visible. Rather, the personal is constituted within a web of relations that includes relations of time (how the past works on the present) and relations with others, knowledge and authority. The hide and seek of the personal is played out on this terrain, but its movements may exceed the force of the ideological and the institutional. 91

Does such "excess" constitute transitional space and, concomitantly, the sphere of the personal? Or, as Pitt asks, "How does the personal become, well, personal" (91)? To answer, she turns to Winnicott's exposition of cultural experience as a transitional space. Such a conception suggests that the personal is located not in content that reflects the world. Rather, Pitt offers, the personal is "a method for observing how we experience ourselves in the world" (91).

"An Interminable Undulating Force"

If a method, the play of the personal would appear to be temporal in its structure. After Freud, Pitt points out that traumatic events can only be approached by means of deferred revision, what he termed *Nachträglichkeit*. It is "the interminable undulating force of *Nachträglichkeit*" (98) that intrigues Pitt, its movement in psychoanalytic life-history making, movement enabling us to notice "how we find and lose sight of our capacity to apprehend what matters most to us: the surprise of intersection between our movements onward and our detours back" (98).

The notion of "detour" implies that we cannot proceed straight on. Rather, we are forced (lured?) to leave our path, required to work on our selves indirectly, and in the time apparently lost—Nachträglichkeit—we revise our direction, relocate our path, reassemble our selves. Does "detour," in fact, name our path, specifically its divergence from the official route, in excess of the ideological and the institutional? Is this transitional space between interiority (as Winnicott's secret self) and exteriority (as the public sphere) a gap that, for Pitt, is the site of pedagogy? If the curriculum is comprised of cultural representations, to teach we must dwell in the gap between the institutional and the ideological, the space in excess of them. Perhaps, then, in the transitional spaces—the gaps—between interiority and exteriority, we can discern "the play of the personal."

In my intellectual life history, the "personal" became compelling before my engagement with feminist theory and gender studies, before the phase of "coming out," during which time "the play of the personal" became, for me, revolutionary. For many women, the two events occurred simultaneously (see Pinar et al. 1995, chapter 10, section III). As Pitt notes, Jane Gallop attributes the scholarly interest in the personal to feminism. Insofar as the private spaces and public sites of gender have been traumatizing, gender has animated both men's and women's efforts to occupy and articulate "the personal," that (pedagogical) gap between interiority and exteriority.

After Shoshana Felman, Pitt asks what it means to read and write autobiographically from traumatic sites of subjectivity and, specifically, from the trauma of being a woman in a patriarchal culture. She quotes Felman's dramatic assertion "that none of us, as woman, has as yet, precisely, an autobiography" (see 99) noting how counterintuitive the claim seems, given the power of women's autobiographies, the extensive feminist scholarship on autobiography, not to mention "the tremendous pleasure many of us experience when we read women's autobiographies" (99).

Pitt finds Felman's approach to women's autobiography resonant with Sarah Kofman's observation that philosophical and theoretical studies have often functioned as detours that point the way to women's autobiography. Felman argued that women's autobiography "must pass through the detours of literature and theory," and, "moreover, [that] literature and theory must pass through the detours of autobiography" (see 99). But Felman's essays are not autobiographical in any traditional sense, Pitt notes; they do not narrate a life history. Rather, they narrate the autobiography of a reading practice, a distinctive reading practice characterized by "the reconstitutive tracing of self-implication," a tracing reminiscent, in Deborah Britzman's (1995) memorable phrase, of not reading straight. Such a reading practice, such tracing, Pitt suggests, discloses "the force, the significance, and surprise of Nachträglichkeit" (100).

"[I]t becomes clear that we cannot think of the 'personal' as something we possess," Pitt points out. "Rather," she continues, "the personal emerges as a dynamic that is made in performance and remade within the work of interpretation" (121). Sometimes such "performance" represents "resistance." To illustrate (calling on Keyssar and Gallop), Pitt notes that a male student who refuses to behave properly might well perceive the role of student as gendered, as feminized. For such a student, to "behave" requires a transgendering performance. There is, of course, nothing wrong with that.

For Chodorow, at least in Gallop's view, "individuation is itself gendered male" (see 121). In this view, the mother/daughter symbiosis is judged as pre-social and then restructured by the masculinist world of the social. If the pre-oedipal phase is feminized, what is the gender of the "secret self" that Winnicott imagines? What are the gender and sexuality of the communicational play of "hide-and-seek"? Is it heterosexual? Is autobiographical confession by definition a feminized activity, positioning one as the feminized patient, animated by one's suffering to seek recognition from the (male) Master? Or, given the apparent impossibility of this communicational aspiration, does the therapeutic encounter provide an opportunity for hiding as well as seeking, for protecting the "secret self" safe in (mis)recognition? Is the feminized patient triumphant in the dissolution of the Master's position that his failure to alleviate feminized suffering precipitates?

If autobiographical confession is a feminized and feminizing project, is that why when many "men" practiced autobiography, they were compelled to deny their libidinal relational currents of dependency by fabricating an "individuated" identity separate from and independent of others? Is this the genesis, then, of the fantasy of the "self-made man," that compensatory model of nineteenth-century (white) manhood that lingers still today? Do such split-off (and self-divided) male egos guarantee the multiplication of "others," repudiated contents of the white male mind politically subjugated in concrete lives of disavowed alterity?

Idealization and Alterity

After Kaja Silverman, Pitt asks us "to imagine a subject whose capacity to idealize can combine with a susceptibility to culture to work against the logic of incorporation and, at the same time, toward the idealization of socially repudiated bodies" (77). Pitt points out that "idealization, if it is to become a tool for political cinema, must take the form of enhancing, not self-love, but rather loving relations with others" (80).

Combining Lacan's notion of "self" as structured from within and the Wallon-Silverman view that it is structured "at-a-distance" allows us, Pitt notes, to understand how the ego recognizes another subject as separate from itself. This potential of intersubjective recognition, she continues, is crucial, for it allows Silverman to imagine "a politically productive relation to bodily otherness," built upon processes of identification that are "exteriorizing rather than interiorizing" (78) Pitt points out:

> This other subject, apprehended as both near and at-a-distance, can be idealized as "good" or "beautiful" even if it does not possess the features that would make it a good candidate for affirming and elaborating the ideal ego. Moreover, when the logic of identification proceeds along a trajectory of exteriorization, the image that is reflected back to the viewer is not assimilated to the self and thus retains the features of its own corporal singularity. 79

This is what late nineteenth-century southern white men were unable—and unwilling—to do, and so they misrecognized black men as the sexual predators they themselves were (Pinar 2001). Of course, processes of exteriorized identification cannot proceed apart from interior psychic contents and processes; Pitt observes that Silverman does not overlook the dangers of idealizing forms of love that exalt the object. In my example, nineteenth-century southern white men exalted southern white women; their positioning of white women on pedestals of the "saintly mother" and the "gracious wife" left them imprisoned within domestic cells fashioned by white men's imagination, enforced by white men's laws.

Pitt points to Silverman's description of the ways in which ideal images play a role in facilitating relations to all love objects, as these "create a space for theorizing love as a gift that can be bestowed on identities who are idealized from afar and, hence, in relations that locate the desires of wanting to be or wanting to have the other within a broader range of social markers of idealization and de-idealization" (79). Those nineteenth-century "ladies" who became "women"—for instance, suffragists—were indeed de-idealized, scorned by men who were unable to perceive women apart from their "place" in men's self-split imagination.

"If ideality is to be conferred at-a-distance," Pitt writes, "students need opportunities to engage with materials that call attention to—even as they disrupt—identificatory practices that are aligned with normative practices" (82). After Silverman (and Maxine Greene, I might add), Pitt suggests that imaginative works may prove to be more influential than we assume "in creating the conditions for learning about social hatreds and discriminations" (82). Art, she seems to be suggesting, works at the level of fantasy and thereby encourages the elaboration and expansion of the ego's libidinal attachments. Indeed, the political potential of art may reside more in its structures of fantasy than in its verisimilitude.

It may be, Pitt theorizes, that we require the aesthetic experience of the world-not-yet (a beautiful, future wherein social difference animates rather than disturbs human intersubjectivity) before we can conduct ourselves ethically with others. "The psychoanalytic subject," Pitt underscores, "is an effect of its libidinal ties to others" (71). "Simply put," she concludes (beautifully), "the surface of the self is not there, waiting to be fully experienced by the developing individual; it is, rather, more like a work of art that comes into being as the effects of touching and being touched, seeing and being seen" (74).

But, Pitt notes, "we seem to be less clear about the complicated ways in which people attach or do not attach to knowledge and how these attachments turn into actions" (75). Nor, may I add, do we seem very interested in providing public-school students with many opportunities to explore these attachments, as the predetermined curriculum with its standardized results obliterates any possibility of personal attachment. Presumably that is reserved for graduate school, an experience relatively few public-school students (and not all graduate students) experience. For the rest, knowledge remains unattached, split-off from lived experience, free-floating like the anxiety Freud's female patients sometimes suffered.

Unspeakable Suffering
Mastery and Destitution

Because the female patient (Pitt discusses the case of Irma) gave Freud her resistance, the patient/doctor relationship was radically altered. Resisted, stymied, Freud was no longer the Master, not of the cure, not of the patient, not of the illness. After Felman, Pitt suggests that the "fecundity" of the psychoanalytic relationship proceeds, in fact, from the destruction of the doctor's (Freud's) mastery, from what Felman terms "the destitution, in effect, of mastery as such" (see 111). Is this destitution a version of Silverman's (1992) "male subjectivity at the margins" or Bersani's (1987, 1995) ecstatic "self-shattering" that he associates with anal sex, with being penetrated by the Other, thereby becoming Other to oneself? Does the fecundity of the analytic—and pedagogical?—relationship follow from the (male) doctor's (teacher's) structural performance of the "crisis of masculinity," a crisis that enables the (feminized) patient to experience her own (masculinized?) unconscious, surfacing as resistance, sinking the "ship" that is the doctor's self-sealed sense of mastery?

This reading of what constitutes a psychic event within the psychoanalytic session—that it follows from "transformed power relations between (male) doctors and their (female) patients"—is congruent, Pitt suggests, with Lacan's own understanding of the psychoanalytic dialogue. The altered power relations between doctor and patient transformed the psychoanalytic dialogue into an exchange between two individuals who are both self-divided, and whose communication—through hide-and-seek?—occurs through their self-division. Such a structure of communication inaugurates psychoanalysis as a theory and as a method of self-analysis. Such a structure, for Felman, originates in Freud's identification with his female patient and her "unspeakable suffering."

Felman seems to be suggesting, Pitt suggests, that as long as such suffering remains a "nodal point" of psychoanalysis, fundamental questions of gender (what does a woman want?) and understanding (itself gendered in psychoanalysis as what Freud, or the [male] doctor, wants) remain unresolved, knotted, or conflated in "femininity," both the site and expression of resistance and desire. It is to Lacan's work that Pitt turns to underscore that the "desire" for understanding becomes a trap of the ego, an inviting trap both for psychoanalytic theory and for its participants.

Pitt notes that it is this desire to be understood, as a woman, by her male analyst that prompted Felman to write her essay on Freud. While Felman found her listener "caring, compassionate and astute," she also found him lacking, unable to understand her as a woman. "Felman's wish to be understood as a woman by a man is structured," Pitt writes, "like the plea of the hysteric who addresses her question about what it means to be a woman precisely to the one who cannot give her what she wants and then lets him know that she is not, will not be satisfied" (see 112). Addressed to an imagined Master (the teacher?), the analyst (Freud?) who declined (failed in) the position, unable to meet the expectation of understanding the very position (structured by the plea, animated by suffering) demands. Does the "destitution" of "mastery" enable the patient to retrieve the Otherness of the analyst as her own lived "nodal point"? In the destitution of his mastery—the "crisis" of masculinity now played out—does the castrated analyst now claim his self-difference, his identification as "woman" as well as as "man"?

Pitt juxtaposes Freud's famous question "What does woman want?" with Lacan's famous pronouncement "La femme n'existe pas." Are these two questions not related? (Pitt allows that Lacan's assertion does not "exceed the structure of Freud's question" [113].) Is not the question Freud posed (also) self-addressed? In addition to his desire to address and to relieve the suffering of the gendered Other, is he not (also), like the feminized patient, trying to reclaim his (Adam's) "rib" (a myth that cannot conceive of "woman" apart from His relation to Her), inaugurating self-difference and internalized otherness? Because the mode of address—hysteria and unspeakable suffering—requires the fantasy of the Master (a fantasy that obliterates the gendered formation of "woman"), does it also castrate, make destitute, render Him now hysterical and outside the patriarchal structure in which He might imagine Himself capable of satisfying feminized desire?

Is this mode of address embedded in historical forms of autobiographical practice, as feminist theorists such as Leigh Gilmore (1994) have suggested? Pitt seems to say so, noting, in response to the Lacanian assertion (that la femme n'existe pas) that "perhaps she [woman] does not [exist], at least not quite in the way much feminist writing has wished" (113). Pitt notes that Felman did not know how her project was also a testimony to her own autobiography as missing: missing because, she writes, "I still could not essentially address it to myself—truly address it, that is, to a woman" (see 117).

An Unyielding Knot

Not only does "woman" not "exist," it appears neither does the "child." Pitt examines Winnicott's claim that there is no such thing as a baby. For Winnicott, "There is no such thing as an infant, meaning, of course, that whenever one finds an infant, one finds maternal care, and without maternal care there would be no infant" (119). As in childhood, as in psychoanalysis, as in education, Pitt asserts that "the breakdowns of meaning that occur between two subjects are necessary for the development of the individual" (119).

Pitt reminds us that Lacan's account of the mirror stage theorizes the infant's apprehension of "self" as installed at the moment of self-recognition in the image reflected by the mirror. This is, Pitt underlines, also a misrecognition, and she notes that, for Lacan, this structure of self-(mis)recognition effects the split subject. Drawing too on Wallon's work, Pitt points out that this process is not "instantaneous." Rather, "self-recognition is a culminating rather than inaugurating event" (78).

"The knot of the unknown that resists interpretation" (106), Pitt acknowledges, is what Freud termed the "navel" of the dream. Is the "secret self" the knot of the self-system that guarantees self-(mis)recognition and self-difference? Are the meanings of the dream and the meaning of the "self" both beyond interpretation or only resistant to it? If "hide-and-seek" accurately describes the movements of interiority and exteriority, does the former hide while the latter seeks? Is Winnicott's "secret self" also Lacan's Real, in which case one's very capacity for interpretation, even for resistance, must necessarily, inevitably, break down? Is our seeking a hiding from the incoherence and unintelligibility of the Real? This would seem to be implied in Pitt's observation that "It is this failure of the ego to maintain its coherence that Lacan links to the subject's quest for signification set into motion by a terrifying encounter with the real" (107).

In this scenario, the journey toward communication—intersubjective intelligibility and recognition—is animated by hysteria, a terror of the unspeakable and unknowable. Pitt relies on Colette Soler to situate Lacan's distinction between the ego—that is, the sum of identifications—and the speaking subject, the "self" who comes into being and indeed must be made to appear through speech. Is this process, in part, an instance of Althusserian interpellation, in which the subject is hailed into existence by the "Other," (mis)recognizing itself in its identification with the Other's signification?

Self-formation involves learning how to position oneself in the place of the cause of one's own desire, Pitt tells us. If so, such learning, precisely because it involves learning, dissolves narcissism, unself-conscious as that state is. Such learning engages one in "the interminable struggle to symbolize the cause of desire" (108), a primal force whose tip may not break the water's surface. There can be no fantasy of avoiding the "iceberg"—is that psychic fact one cause of the enduring fascination with the Titanic?—and not because there is insufficient time. It is because there is no time in advance; the project of learning occurs afterward and through peering through the opaque depths of the unconscious up toward a surface refracted unevenly, free-associatively. In this interpretive sense time is always past, even when it appears before us. We cannot avoid the "iceberg" because we have already "sunk." It is already after the tragedy that we find ourselves subjugated, suffering, asking for recognition from Him who cannot see us apart from himself, by whom we could not bear being seen anyway. Still, we demand to know, to understand: was our demise avoidable? Is it decipherable? Perhaps if it had not been our maiden voyage, we rue. Surely we can raise ourselves from the ocean floor. Is this the fantasy of free-association, a technique that takes us back before the "collision" with the Real, before demise?

Effort at such learning—"this autobiography of learning" as Pitt puts it—"takes place in the strange time of *Nachträglichkeit*" (108). It is "a time," she suggests, "that is neither representation nor identity but difference and self-difference" (111). "What Freud seems to be circling around," Pitt concludes, "is the notion that, at the very center of relations between education and psychoanalysis, lies an unyielding knot" (14). It is no doubt true, as Pitt asserts, that "the productivity of this version of subjectivity and its implications for theorizing all manner of relations within teaching and learning have yet to be fully realized" (108). It is Pitt's work here that helps us believe in such productivity by so significantly contributing to it.

I have only circled around the knotted complexity of Alice Pitt's remarkable book. As this provocative and important work underscores, there is no tradition of systematic inquiry into the sphere of the subjective, into the processes of self-formation—and their complex and ever-changing relations to the social and historical—that offers us as many conceptual tools as do the various strands of psychoanalytic theory. In the broad field of education—in which curriculum theory is situated—there is a long if attenuated tradition of interest in psychoanalysis. During the Progressive Era in the United States, efforts to theorize a psychoanalysis of education were initiated (see, for instance, Cremin 1961, 209ff.), but these disappeared as "business thinking" and the "national interest" dominated school curriculum and the scholarship surrounding it.

In our time there is a renaissance of scholarly interest in psychoanalysis in education, led by Deborah Britzman (1998), Stephen Appel (1999), Doug Aoki (2002), Wendy Atwell-Vasey (1998a, 1998b), jan jagodzinski (2002), and Alice Pitt. It is also evident in a number of important studies not exclusively or even primarily psychoanalytic in orientation, among them Madeleine Grumet's (1988) study of women and teaching, Alan Block's (1997) theorization of the school's psychological violence against the child, in Marla Morris' (2001) research on curriculum and the Holocaust, and in Julie Webber's (in press) exposition of school violence.

I too have employed psychoanalytic theory—a version of object relations theory (see Chodorow 1978)—in my effort to understand the gender of racial politics and violence in America (2001). It was psychoanalytic theory that enabled me to appreciate—however incipiently—the "queer" dimensions of racial subjugation. It is psychoanalytic theory—and, specifically, Alice Pitt's sophisticated and subtle performance of it—that enables us to appreciate the play of the personal and the complexity of the conversation that is the curriculum.

References

Aoki, Douglas Sadao (2002, Spring). The price of teaching: Love, evasion, and the subordination of knowledge. JCT: Journal of Curriculum Theorizing (18) 1, 21–39.

Appel, Stephen (Ed.). (1999). Psychoanalysis and pedagogy. Westport, CT: Bergin & Garvey.

Atwell-Vasey, Wendy (1998a). Nourishing words: Bridging private reading and public teaching. Albany: State University of New York Press.

Atwell-Vasey, Wendy (1998b). Psychoanalytic feminism and the powerful teacher. In William F. Pinar (Ed.), Curriculum: Toward New Identities (143–156). New York: Garland.

Bersani, Leo (1987). Is the rectum a grave? October 43, 197–222.

Bersani, Leo (1995). Homos. Cambridge, MA: Harvard University Press.

Block, Alan (1997). I'm only bleeding: Education as the practice of social violence against the child. New York: Peter Lang.

Britzman, Deborah P. (1995). Is there a queer pedagogy? Or, stop reading straight. Educational Theory 45 (2), 151–165.

Britzman, Deborah P. (1998). Lost subjects, contested objects: Toward a psychoanalytic inquiry of learning. Albany, NY: State University of New York Press.

Chodorow, Nancy J. (1978). The reproduction of mothering. Berkeley: University of California Press.

Cremin, Lawrence A. (1961). The transformation of the school: Progressivism in American education, 1876–1957. New York: Alfred A. Knopf.

Gilmore, Leigh (1994). Autobiographics: A feminist theory of women's self-representation. Ithaca, NY: Cornell University Press.

Grumet, Madeleine R. (1988). Bitter milk: Women and teaching. Amherst: University of Massachusetts Press.

jagodzinski, jan (Ed.) (2002). Pedagogical desire: Authority, seduction, transference, and the question of ethics. Westport, CT: Bergin & Garvey.

Langeveld, M. (1983a). The stillness of the secret place. Phenomenology + Pedagogy, 1 (1), 11–17.

Langeveld, M. (1983b). The secret place in the life of the child. Phenomenology + Pedagogy, 1 (2), 181–191.

Morris, Marla (2001).Holocaust and Curriculum. Mahwah, NJ: Lawrence Erlbaum.

Pinar, William F. (2001). The gender of racial politics and violence in America: Lynching, prison rape, and the crisis of masculinity. New York: Peter Lang.

Pinar, William F., Reynolds, William M., Slattery, Patrick, Taubman, Peter M. (1995). Understanding curriculum. New York: Peter Lang.

Pitt, Alice (2003). The play of the personal: Psychoanalytic narratives of feminist education. New York: Peter Lang.

Silverman, Kaja (1992). Male subjectivity at the margins. New York & London: Routledge.
Webber, Julie A. (in press). Failure to hold: Politics, proto-citizenship and school violence. Landham, MD: Rowman & Littlefield.

Acknowledgments

"What," asks Adam Phillips (2000, 296), "does the analyst want for the patient that the patient can at least hope for from the analyst?" As is so often the case with Phillips, what happens next is less the formation of an answer to his provocative question than a meditation on what we might lose if we were to settle upon an answer. Is there something about the analysis of some thing—in the case of psychoanalysis, the dream, the unconscious or the defense—that ruins our pleasure for questions, for looking elsewhere, for falling in love? I have been lucky to have met up with teachers who are not only interested in their students' questions but also in what it means to find and lose the capacity to make questions from one's learning. Roger Simon and Deanne Bogdan are exemplary at keeping open that curious space between what the teacher wants for the student and what the student can hope for from the teacher. They have also commented usefully, provocatively, and astutely on the space, providing a rich language for thinking about it as well as a nourishing environment for experiencing it. I am also grateful for the conversations on curriculum theory and what it can hope for that Bill Pinar has worked so hard to provoke and then keep moving over many years, and I am delighted by the opportunity to publish in one of his series. I want to thank him particularly for his insightful preface. He points to a thicket of interconnections, returns, and persistent preoccupations that I had either not ever noticed or had skipped over in my hurry to get somewhere else. Sometimes, as I argue in the first chapter, a return is what it takes to begin to look elsewhere, which is not the same thing as getting there. The conversation continues.

Others have joined in the conversation and have generously read and commented on my work at various times in its development. I am grateful for the intellectual friendship of Don Dippo, Pat Elliot, Bill Haver, Patti Lather, Jane Miller, Judith Robertson, Dennis Sumara, Sharon Todd, and Dan Yon. I continue to learn both from and about psychoanalysis, education and feminism from talented graduate students: Chloë Brushwood-Rose, Angela Failler, Jen Gilbert, Colette Granger, and Jessica Ringrose. Maggie Breau and Bianca Rus tended to the details of editing with keen eyes and sufficient humor to weather various technological cloudbursts. Bianca also asked astute conceptual questions disguised as editorial observations. Chris Meyers, Sophie Appel, an anonymous copy editor from Peter Lang Publishers and Asa Weinstein have all been delightful to work with as this manuscript has been turned into a book.

Closer to home, I want to thank Peggy Pitt and the late Douglas Pitt for being the kind of parents who frustrated their children's wishes in just the right doses and who never concealed or withheld their love. Most of all I thank Deborah Britzman who can play all of the parts I assign her in fantasy and survive. She is my best reader and best everything.

Several chapters were published elsewhere, and I thank Taylor and Francis Journals (See *http://www.tandf.co.uk)* for permission to reprint the following:

"Qualifying Resistance: Some Comments on Methodological Dilemmas" from *QSE: International Journal of Qualitative Studies in Education*, 11(4), 1998.

"Love Stories: Cinematic Lures and Identification from Afar" from *Review of Education, Pedagogy, Cultural Studies*, 20(1), 1998.

"Hide and Seek: The Play of the Personal in Education" from *Changing English: Studies in Reading and Culture*, 7(1), 2000.

"The Dreamwork of Autobiography: Felman, Freud, and Lacan" from *Feminist Engagements: Reading, Resisting, and Revisioning Male Theorists in Education and Cultural Studies*, edited by Kathleen Weiler, 2001. Reproduced by permission of Routledge, Inc, also part of the Taylor and Francis Group.

This work has been supported by the Social Sciences and Humanities Research Council of Canada under the auspices of "Difficult Knowledge in Teaching and Learning in the University: A Psychoanalytic Inquiry" (410-98-1028). The views expressed are those of the author.

Chapter One

Narrating Implication: From Resistance to Autobiography

> It is in psychic sleeping that the self hatches, sponsors and cultivates unconscious creativity, such as preparing the night's dream, or working on an essay before a topic is known, or ...
>
> —Christopher Bollas, *Hysteria*

Prologue

Psychic sleeping intrigues me, and Bollas' open-ended sentence gives me pleasure even if I am not sure I fully understand what he means. Referring neither to a full fall into sleep, where dreams do occur, nor to the concentrated state of wakefulness, where essays get written, psychic sleeping is the name Bollas gives to the kind of work the mind does that remains elusive and obscure. Psychic sleeping, he suggests, is an achievement; it can be inhibited, thwarted, overruled, and stunted by the mind's overwork on other tasks. We might think of learning as one of the outcomes of psychic sleeping, but an appetite for learning also sets psychic sleep going, providing the raw material.

There is a more personal resonance at play here. Working on an essay before the topic is known is not an uncommon experience for me, and behind this chapter lies an even greater than usual number of "sub-files" containing half-starts, discarded bits that have wandered off in new directions, and pages and pages of beginnings that seem to defer endlessly that difficult task of thinking an idea through to some commitment. This creative though frustrating process requires the touchstones of prior learning to get going, but one must also learn—if the essay is ever to be readied for an audience—what the topic is. Learning is a curious process, both coming up from the rear and leaping ahead of the self who learns. The question is "How do we learn?" That may best be contemplated as requiring an attentiveness to two times, the past tense and the future anterior, that work through and even on each other. Perhaps the notion of psychic sleeping, as learning's incubation in this curious tense that has no name, can help us imagine some new ways of thinking about what learning is, and, following from this, the pedagogical conditions that nourish it and research methods that are up to the task of commenting upon it

Marks of Missed Meaning

> Lacan's writing read like Mallarmé's—an obscure and enigmatic, yet powerful and effective, poetic prose. It appealed to me the way literature appeals to me: without my being able to make immediate sense of it or translate it, I was made to take in and absorb more than I knew.
>
> —Shoshana Felman, *Jacques Lacan and the Adventure of Insight*

> In analytic discourse, you presume the subject of the unconscious to be capable of reading. This is what the whole affair of the unconscious amounts to. Not only do you presume him to be capable of reading, but you presume him to be capable of learning how to read.
>
> —Jacques Lacan, *cited in Felman, Jacques Lacan and the Adventure of Insight*

Shoshana Felman (1987) urges us to distinguish between application and implication when it comes to psychoanalytic theory and its uses: "The practice of psychoanalysis (as well as the experience of a practical reading) is a process, not a set of doctrines. In the process, one can *implicate* the doctrines, one can perhaps imply them, not apply them" (11, italics in original). In my well-used copy of her book, a thick pencilled line wraps around these sentences and their immediate neighbors. The word key appears in the margin. These bold gestures belie a long struggle to make useful sense of Felman's insistence, to make meaning from her advice in spite of the immediacy of its appeal to my field of curriculum theory, where the relationship between theory and practice is a constant source of concern, complaint and invention. Upon this return to a text I thought I knew, I am surprised by her wording: "to implicate the doctrines" now leaps off the page as a bit of unfinished business.

Somewhat belatedly, I approach, from another angle, Felman's project of thinking psychoanalysis and pedagogy (or education) together. This other angle follows my history of learning since my first encounter with Felman and Lacan. As will become clearer a bit further on, my use of the term belated to describe coming to write about my history of learning is tied to the psychoanalytic concept of *Nachträglichkeit*, translated by James Strachey as "deferred action" and discussed more thoroughly in Chapter Six. One of the difficulties I have confronted in writing this chapter has to do with trying to think and write psychoanalytically about my own learning. The radical lesson psychoanalysis offers about learning is, according to Felman, that it proceeds "through breakthroughs, leaps, discontinuities, regressions, and deferred action" (76). This view constructs learning as difficult to pin down and even to pinpoint. How, for example, can we tell the difference between a leap away from and a leap toward learning? Grappling with questions posed by a psychoanalytic theory of learning means, in ways that I have only recently begun to appreciate, acknowledging difficulties in constructing narratives of learning that are up to the task of representing the significance one makes from encounters with knowledge and with those who represent knowledge (see Pitt & Britzman In press).

Moreover, unlike Felman, who describes herself as a student of literature and psychoanalysis, a position that clearly informs her own narration of learning quoted above, I am a student of education and psychoanalysis. My history of learning is implicated in very different ways from hers. The "doctrines" I explore, from the vantage of psychoanalytic lessons of implication, are not the doctrines of psychoanalysis nor of literary criticism; rather they are the residual effects of my learning and unlearning from critical and feminist educational studies and from psychoanalytic theories of learning and subjectivity. My surprise at the marks I have left in a book that played an important role in my intellectual development suggests that they might hold clues for exploring this intimate history. Mary Jacobus (1999), likening reading to eating, considers what it means to leave things on the plate:

> Who hasn't recently defaced a book—succumbing to the temptation to mark a difficult or significant page, line by line, paragraph by paragraph? Who hasn't mutilated a paperback by turning down the corner of a page, or read and reread a particularly obscure passage (by Derrida, for instance—or even Freud?). Missed meanings haunt us. (30)

Jacobus describes a reading practice not fully present to itself. There is indeed something ambiguous about meaning that is not available and yet makes itself felt if only by virtue of ghostly presence. How do textual meanings and readers miss each other? There may be a gap in the reader's knowledge. George Steiner (1980), in a discussion of the difficulties encountered in reading poetry, calls these kinds of obstacles contingent difficulties that can be overcome by further study or homework. He identifies three more categories of difficulty: modal difficulties concern the problem of relevance to the reader; tactical difficulties lie within the poem as representations of a conflict between innermost meaning and public statements; finally, ontological difficulties are met when the poem calls attention to the very possibility of understanding and communication as we know it.

These are useful categories for thinking about missed meaning, but psychoanalytic orientation to reading looks elsewhere, beginning with the reader rather than with what is read. It points to the psychical conflict in the reader that is set into motion by reading. There is something about meaning that is distressing to the reader, but there must also be something about this distress that excites or incites the reader. Otherwise, why be haunted? For Felman, missing meaning is an active process of resistance to what meaning proposes to or provokes in the reader. "Ignorance," she writes, "is nothing other than the desire to ignore: its nature is less cognitive than performative" (79). Missed meaning, Felman suggests, holds an intolerable significance for the reader. It haunts us because it matters to us, but, like an apparition, it remains elusive, felt but not quite perceived. Missed meaning draws us back to the scene, and in the return lies the potential to move missed meaning from obscurity to significance. The chapters that follow tell one kind of story about my learning from psychoanalysis and education. Being surprised by one's own underlined bits and marginal exhortations suggests that another story can be made of missed meaning. This story is belated and is marked by the difference between learning and representing learning.

Using Felman's study of Lacan and Freud's pedagogy and the psychoanalytic theory of resistance, I have explored the significance of learning from students' resistance to knowledge, in particular, feminist knowledges, as well as methodological issues raised by my research. In this chapter, following the clues of missed meaning left in the margins, I turn to "the tangles of implication," a phrasing borrowed from Deborah Britzman (1997), arising from the risk of psychoanalytic interpretation in educational research. One theme running throughout psychoanalytically informed educational research concerns a paradox that might go something like this: we cannot know the unconscious, our own or others', and yet our understanding of how people do and do not learn is deeper and, I would argue, more ethical when we begin with the assumption that learning is a psychic event that, like a dream, consists of both conscious and unconscious processes.

What is the status of psychoanalytically informed interpretation in the context of educational research? Perhaps this question is too condensed. Taking one step back, we can wonder what kind of activity interpretation is in educational research. Following from this, we can ask: What kind of work do we expect from interpretation? What does interpretation do? These questions are provoked by the pushes and pulls between two impulses in critical educational research, both of which call into question interpretation as the authoritative bestowal of meaning on events, experience, or texts. Research that explores in greater depth the lived experiences of groups of people historically marginalized within education in order to affect educational policy, practices, and institutional structures seeks to transform knowledge about such groups by eliciting, directly or indirectly, their perspectives. Here meaning is made from experience, and interpretation is tied to and expressed by identity. In this view, the gap between identity and its meaning is an effect of power.

A second impulse follows from poststructural theories of language and subjectivity to consider the effects of power, knowledge, and language on individuals' narratives about their lived experience. Narratives of experience, from this perspective, are valuable, not primarily for their capacity to illuminate alternative understandings of how the world works, but, rather, because they permit exploration of the *a priori* subject positions available to individuals and investigation of how those positions are taken up and resisted, thus potentially reproducing or disrupting existing power relations. Here meaning is made from discourses of power and knowledge, and interpretation locates the traces power/knowledge leaves in texts, utterances, and institutional arrangements and practices. Interpretation also reveals interruptions in the coherence of dominant discourses. The gap between identity, now conceived as subjectivity, and meaning points to the non-unitary nature of discourse and to the fragmentation of experience across a range of discursive positions.

Initially I saw my work as being grounded in the second orientation, but an interest in noticing the similarities between the dynamics set in motion by psychoanalytic dialogue and those of teaching and learning has also meant thinking about the dimensions of meaning that escape discourse and discourse effects, residing instead in unconscious wishes and fantasy. I want to consider, in more explicit ways, what it means to learn about and from education and psychoanalysis and what it is to make meaning from that experience. I begin by noting my vexed relationship to personal narratives. In spite of my commitment to the ethical, epistemological, and political value of developing knowledge that begins with the perspectives of groups of people fighting for social equality, civil rights, and the cultural right to narrate their history, I remain deeply suspicious of the use of stories of personal experience as the grounds of knowledge, as an explanatory device for understanding experience, or even as a bridge between students and the curriculum or between the teacher and her students.

My suspicion is shored up by the poststructuralist theories of language and subjectivity referred to above that invert the relationship between language and the subject, insisting that experience be viewed as an artifact of language, power, and discourses of knowledge rather than their source. A pedagogical hesitation follows from noticing how personal narratives of experience can be used to foreclose rather than open discussion and debate.

Yet, as I review the essays included in this book, I am taken aback by the extent to which various kinds of personal narratives do figure in my work and animate my thinking. Even my title, in a somehow tangled way, contains both personal and narrative. Yet this too is a conundrum: narratives raise and settle the problem of the personal. So, while the individual narratives, whether gathered as data or encountered as texts, speak to me in compelling ways, my engagement with them does not conform to either model of interpretation mentioned above. I neither assume that narratives speak for themselves as representatives of identity, nor am I satisfied by the notion that discourse can account fully for what matters about stories of experience.[1] Interpretation plays a large role in my work, but the work it does is less to bestow meaning than it is to speculate on possibilities for new ways of thinking about persistent problems or, as in D. W. Winnicott's work, I use interpretation to move things along. In the following chapters, the things I am interested in moving along are the ways we think about teaching, learning, curriculum, and educational research. In this chapter, however, I explore the gap between making and missing meaning as a piece of the generative work of thinking about psychoanalysis and education together.

I approach, in this autobiography of learning, the question of implication as a series of returns. I begin with a return to Felman, going back over her words that I have marked in the text and then forgotten. Travelling between her insistence that we "implicate the doctrines" and the notion that we resist learning precisely where we are most implicated, I consider what I think is at stake in the question of implication as I question my own implication in my learning. The chapter, then, is both a story of learning and a story about the difficulty of narrating learning. It comes at the beginning of this collection of essays but also necessarily after having written them. I return to some of the themes raised here in Chapter Seven.

The Latin root of the verb "to implicate" is *plicare*, to fold. The root is served faithfully in synonyms for the adjective implicated: intertwined, entangled, wrapped up with, involved in. The traces of the root and these synonyms are also evident in three definitions of the verb that appear in my *Oxford Canadian Dictionary* (1998). The first, as hinted in the examples, associates guilt and accusation with involvement: "to show (a person or thing) to be concerned or involved (in a charge, crime, etc)." The second calls upon the passive voice and introduces the idea of being affected in addition to being involved. The third definition points to something emerging as a result of something else: "lead to as a consequence or inference." When Felman speaks about implicating psychoanalytic knowledge, all three meanings are mobilized to create within Lacan's reading of Freud one version of Britzman's "tangles of implication." Felman (1987) cites a passage from a recording of Lacan's 1975 talk at Yale University that neatly summarizes the movement from one moment of implication to another:

> [Freud's] first interest was in hysteria. He spent a lot of time listening, and while he was listening, there resulted something paradoxical, a *reading*. It was while listening to hysterics that he *read* that there was an unconscious. That is, something he could only construct, and in which he himself was implicated; he was implicated in it in the sense that, to his great astonishment, he noticed that he could not avoid participating in what the hysteric was telling him, and that he felt affected by it. Naturally, everything in the resulting rules in which he established the practice of psychoanalysis is designed to counteract this consequence, to conduct things in such a way as to avoid being affected. (22–23, emphasis in original)

The curious and indeed tangled dynamics of implication blur boundaries between self and other, between conscious and unconscious messages, and between objective reality and theoretical construction. Let us pick up the qualities of implication that Lacan folds into his "short history" of the development of psychoanalytic thought.

Freud's construction of the unconscious, from the speech of the hysterics, is a consequence of his listening or, as Lacan suggests, reading. Prior to this interpretive leap, the hysteric's unconscious is, of course, already implicated: it is responsible for the symptoms that express her misery but that exceed her capacity to symbolize meaning to herself and to others. Involvement in the unconscious speech of another, the first definition of implicate, turns on the question of what is reading: it is Freud's unconscious. Felman (1987) writes that Freud was "capable of reading in the hysterical discourse of the Other his own unconscious" (23). Freud (1923a) describes psychoanalytic listening as "[catching] the drift of the patient's unconscious with his own unconscious" (239). How is this a guilty reading? Freud's unconscious, like that of the hysteric, is a repository for intolerable wishes that have been repressed. That Freud's unconscious, a creation of none other than Freud, in addition to that of the hysteric, makes itself felt in the psychoanalytic dialogue and constitutes perhaps the most radical assertion that comes from psychoanalysis. Not only does it introduce a revolutionary way of listening, it also signals "the formation of an *irreducible, structural and 'normal' unconscious* rather than a reducible, temporary and pathological one" (Fletcher 1999, 18, emphasis added).

The psychoanalytic dialogue that proceeds from this discovery is not, however, simply a matter of exchanging readings of unconscious material. The second definition of implication concerns being affected. Freud is affected by the speech of the hysteric as he finds himself inexplicably cajoled into playing the parts assigned to him by his patients. The repetition of unresolved conflicts within the psychoanalytic dialogue (transference) comes to the attention of the analyst by virtue of attending to her own affective response to the exchange (counter-transference). Lacan's final sentence, with its touch of irony, completes the circle of implication that comes from admitting the unconscious as "the inherent, irreducible difference between consciousness and itself" (Felman 1987, 57). Freud's efforts to establish rules to help the analyst avoid being affected repeat, in overlapping arcs, the fate of the unconscious in his own work and in those who come after. Felman names an untranslated essay of Lacan's, entitled "The Freudian Unconscious and Ours," the title of which hints at the impossibility of knowing, once and for all, what the unconscious is or even what it does. As Felman points out, the first part of the title retains ambiguity: is it the concept or Freud's unconscious that shall be compared to our own? As a consequence of the original discovery, this same ambiguity follows psychoanalytic theory and practice into contemporary discussions. In Chapter Six, I return to aspects of the limits of Freud's capacity to untangle his implication in his discovery, but here I want to focus more generally on the ways in which this question of implication is both foundational to the discovery of psychoanalysis and persistently threatening to its development.

Felman takes Lacan's treatment of Edgar Allan Poe's short story, "The Purloined Letter," as an allegory for the tendency to lose the radical quality of Freud's discovery:

> I want to argue that psychoanalytic knowledge (Freud's theory, Lacan's theory, or whatever) is itself necessarily a purloined (lost, displaced, or misplaced) letter: it is never simply there, at our disposal to apply. It is something that we necessarily keep losing and have to keep working at to find again. But we cannot find it (have it) once and for all. Like the purloined letter, psychoanalysis always has to be recovered. (11)

For Felman, it is Lacan who reminds us of this important lesson about psychoanalysis, teaching us, if we will be taught, what the analyst considers to have been purloined from Freud but also misplaced *by Freud*. Certainly Lacan enjoys a great deal of credit for the renewal of interest in psychoanalytic theory in various branches of academic research; he is frequently praised for having rescued psychoanalysis from some of Freud's muddles, sorting out for us what we should keep, what we should throw aside, and how we should understand the rest. Of particular interest to me has been Lacan's role in revitalizing feminist engagements with psychoanalytic theory. Felman takes up "the woman question" in a later work (1993) (see Chapter

Six), but here she is interested in what it is about Freud's discovery that makes it so apt to go missing and what all of this might have to do with reading practices. Her description of Freud's originality and what she calls Lacan's rediscovery give us a clue as to the nature of the "adventure of in-sight" that is psychoanalysis:

> Originality is what comes as a surprise: a surprise not only to others, but also to the self. True originality, in other words, is precisely the way in which a reflexive movement, in returning to and upon itself, in effect subverts itself—finds something other than what it had expected, what it had set out to seek; the way in which the answer is bound in effect to displace the question; the way in which what is revolving, what returns to itself, radically displaces the very point of observation. (67)

This dizzying yet captivating characterization can be read as a metaphor for the unconscious, which surprises and decenters the ego, and as a metaphor for knowledge itself which, of course, is marked by the decentering effects of the unconscious. While true of all knowledge production, this observation is made by psychoanalysis and haunts its development and use in particular ways that are instructive to those of us who think about what it means to be affected by knowledge. Indeed, Lacan's short history suggests a great deal about the qualities of labor that are both foundational to psychoanalysis and implicated in the development of its thought: psychoanalytic theory and practice must also struggle to permit the surprise that is foundational to psychoanalytic discovery (Laplanche 1989). There is a double move on Felman's part, who, we must not forget, emphasizes the literary qualities of Freud's and Lacan's writing as well as their use of literature to formulate psychoanalytic knowledge.

Psychoanalysis cannot be simply applied as a set of techniques because it relies upon the surprise of discovery in each and every instance of practice. It is, as Lacan notes with his characteristic sly humor, a science of the particular (Verhaeghe 2001). Practice and theory engender each other but also subvert each other. At the same time, the capacity for surprise that transforms the analysand also transforms, endlessly, analytic knowledge in ways that can neither be predicted nor finalized. Indeed, as critical readings of Freud (and Lacan) suggest, the stories that can be told about psychoanalytic knowledge always contain more than their authors imagine. Felman gets at this quality in her claim that psychoanalytic knowledge must always be recovered even by those who use it on a daily basis. I think we can also read her insistence that psychoanalytic knowledge must be recovered as a metaphor for learning psychoanalysis, whether as a participant in psychoanalytic treatment or as a reader. Jessica Benjamin (1995) goes to Foucault in order to say something about the nature of psychoanalytic knowledge that also implicates any learner:

> As Foucault said in "What Is an Author?" psychoanalysis represents a model of thought different from the one derived from the natural sciences, in which one thinker may simply overthrow the thinking of another. Rather, it is a discursive field, like Marxism, that is tied to its origins in certain formulations of its creators. "The work of initiators of discursivity is not situated in the space the science defines; rather it is the science, or the discursivity, which refers back to their work as the primary points of reference [coordinates]." It is necessary to "return" to the original texts because distortion and omission are intrinsic to the "act of initiation," and these barriers, which also set up "obstacles that prevent returning to the act of initiation—can only be resolved by a return."(4)

It is here, at the point where the surprise of originality intersects with the excess of knowledge and where the initiator of psychoanalysis meets the initiation of the beginner, that my own story of implication must begin. But, to return to a problem hinted at earlier, how can such a story be told? One problem, as our short history of Freud's discovery intimates, is that surprise meets resistance, and the slow work of undoing resistance also domesticates surprise. Surprise, as a quality of experience, resists narration, but we are left with narrative as a way to communicate the surprise of experience. Missed meaning can be the surprise that subverts meaning and the meaning-maker or reader.

My proposal to explore women's resistance to feminist knowledge was crystallized by my first reading of Felman. This work is described more fully in Chapters Two and Three, which have been developed from my dissertation (1995). Part of the appeal was the promise the project held for mixing up two contradictory ideas that were important to me at the time. In one direction, I was deeply concerned by the potential for pedagogical coercion that was just then being noticed in educational literature on critical and feminist pedagogy (Ellsworth 1989; Lather 1991). The self-reflexive turn in critical pedagogy was taken up somewhat differently in discussions of postsecondary feminist education. This is the second direction, one propelled by the urgency with which questions of race and sexuality had begun to complicate the category of gender and by the exploration of the effects of white and heterosexual women's dominance in the women's movement, feminist knowledge production, and classroom dynamics.

There were overlapping concerns between these two bodies of literature, but the question of resistance meant something quite different in studies that brought poststructuralism into conversation with critical and neo-Marxist theory and in those influenced by feminism. This, then, is the contradiction between these two preoccupations: where resistance in critical pedagogy literature was turning towards the reproduction of unequal power relations within the emancipatory classroom, resistance in feminist classrooms more often referred to exclusionary practices within both academic and grassroots feminism as well as the refusal of dominant students to learn about and from racism and heteronormativity. Both, however, pressed a concept of resistance that had formerly signalled collective forms of opposition to domination into service as a way to explore the refusal to become implicated in such struggles or in the knowledge that supported them. An interest in resistance to counter-hegemonic knowledge and pedagogical efforts was something of a generational question for me, which, of course, means that it is also tied up with my relations with my teachers.

To think of one's implication in knowledge as an issue of generation requires a detour through another set of contradictions, here, the contradictory movements between attachment and individuation that haunt any story of surprise in learning. The study of resistance may have been suggested in part by the theoretical work we encountered as we learned about critical pedagogy and cultural studies. We were influenced by the move away from traditional sociological definitions of identity as a reservoir of social effects of power relations, a move that was prompted by poststructural understandings of the negotiations of subjectivity. Just as Freud's study of the unconscious was affected by his own unconscious, it is impossible to come to the insight that learning passes through resistance without also being affected by resistance.

My narrative of learning is complicated by my own resistance to learning. There is nothing new about the idea that graduate students enter academic worlds already overpopulated with the meanings of others—to recall Bakhtin. Foucault's paradoxical observation that there are obstacles preventing a return to the scene of initiation and that no resolution is possible without such a return may provide a method for thinking through one's history of learning while refusing both the progressivist story, where the gaps are finally filled in, and the story of failure, where the cause of derailed progress is revealed in the workings of power relations. I have located my interest in resistance loosely in a context that acknowledges the intersection between my more personal preoccupations and the discussions and debates I joined. Now I want to tell a different kind of story, one that follows a series of returns to their points of my resistance. The first return concerns a persistent effort to develop in educational theory a pedagogy that transcends transmission models. This return links Felman's interest in the pedagogy of psychoanalysis to an orientation that was influential in my own education. A second return takes me to an essay written about eros and desire in the teacher/student relationship. Here I consider the gap between theorizing and experiencing an education that takes up the pedagogical imperative of self-implication.

The Strange Intimacy of Transmission

Felman describes her method of teasing out the pedagogical implications of psychoanalysis and literature as an alternative to what she finds most prevalent in discussions of the relationship between education and psychoanalysis. There is a tendency, she argues, to become mired in what Freud or other representatives of psychoanalytic theory have said *about* education. It is important to remember that most of Freud's references to education are expansive, frequently making little or no distinction between child rearing and formal schooling of the young. For Felman, the logic of commentary that responds to Freud's discussions of education leads in one of two directions: some argue for limiting the repressive force of education by way of more liberal methods, while others (Felman refers here to Catherine Millot [1979]) think of psychoanalysis as an anti-pedagogy that seeks to undo the inevitable detrimental effects of education. From the point of view of psychoanalysis, it seems that education inflicts more harm than good. Of course, things are not that straightforward.

In an essay written towards the end of his life, one of seven comprising the *New Introductory Lectures on Psycho-Analysis* (1932), Freud claims to have left the promise of the first approach to his daughter and successor, child analyst and teacher, Anna Freud. Freud's own life work seems better described by the latter approach as demonstrated by his references to psychoanalysis as a *Nacherziehung* or an after-education (see Britzman In press). I return to the question of what comes first if psychoanalysis comes after. It is trickier than it looks. Let us follow Freud a bit further in this essay as he elaborates his view on the relationship between psychoanalysis and education.

Freud lets his imagination roam towards an alternative formulation of before and after as he considers the recent successes of child analysis and wonders if "it would not be expedient to come to a child's help with an analysis even if he shows no signs of a disturbance, as a measure of safeguarding his health..." (148). What would militate against a prophylactic use of psychoanalysis? Two difficulties come immediately to his mind: the negative attitude towards psychoanalysis by the majority of parents and the "constitution of society" (149). Freud wants to talk about something else. He changes tack and raises yet a third difficulty:

> Let us make ourselves clear as to what the first task of education is. The child must learn to control his instincts. It is impossible to give him liberty to carry out all his impulses without restriction. To do so would be a very instructive experiment for child psychologists; but life would be impossible for the parents and the children themselves would suffer grave damage, which would show itself partly at once and partly in later years. Accordingly education must inhibit, forbid and suppress, and this it has abundantly seen to in all periods of history. But we have learnt from analysis that precisely this suppression of instincts involves the risk of neurotic illness....Thus education has to find its way between the Scylla of non-interference and the Charybdis of frustration. *Unless this problem is entirely insoluble*, an optimum must be discovered which will enable education to achieve the most and damage the least. (149, emphasis added)

There is, of course, more to education than pressuring the instincts, and in other places Freud seems more curious about the formation of libidinal ties and the role they play in propelling the infant, then the child, towards the gratifications of language and knowledge by way of those first others, the parents, who represent the pleasures of these worldly gratifications (see Freud 1914). In this passage, however, Freud does emphasize the considerable risk of education: education must involve the exertion of pressure if the instincts are not to rule the roost, and a possible effect of such pressure is neurotic illness.

Felman suggests that we not confuse the explicit statements Freud and Lacan make about education with their performances as teachers or with the pedagogical implications of psychoanalytic theory and practice. Still she quotes most of this famous passage as she lays the groundwork for two observations about the relationship between psychoanalysis and pedagogy: first, psychoanalysis is from the beginning a critique of education and, second, those of us who come after Freud and Lacan might easily miss what psychoanalysis offers. This is so, she argues, because the legacy of the critique has been reduced to the wish to limit education or its force. Felman omits the portion of the text that I have set into italics. It is indeed a puzzling formulation that fails to cohere syntactically. The problem is not one of translation as the sentence is similarly baffling in the German text.[2] What Freud seems to be circling around is the notion that, at the very center of relations between education and psychoanalysis, lies an unyielding knot. This knot mocks the fragile hope of forging a middle route between freedom and frustration. Thinking back now to the radical discovery that the unconscious is at work in all of us, not only in those who have fallen ill, we might well imagine that Freud is troubled here by the tension between education's exertion of force and our own implication in repression. Certainly, the strangeness of this assertion is reminiscent of the unanalyzable bit at the core of a dream—the navel. This knot troubles the history of the relationship between psychoanalysis and education in ways that both anticipate Felman's contribution but cannot be reduced to the two positions—to limit or to undo the effects of education—that Felman describes as the legacy of psychoanalytic thinking about education.

Deborah Britzman (1998) offers a view of the history of bringing psychoanalysis and education together that is more elaborate than Felman's. Her exploration draws attention to a much larger group of psychoanalysts and educators, and she discusses representatives of different schools of analytic thought, ranging from Freud's contemporaries to our own. Britzman does take seriously what these analysts have to say about education, considering both their observations on the education of children and their struggles to develop their own training institutes. As a point of departure, she traces three co-extensive dynamics that highlight the history of relations between the two fields of inquiry and practice. These include moments:

> (1) when the projects of psychoanalysis and education were posed as indistinguishable; (2) when the project of psychoanalysis was used as a means to critique educational methods; and (3) when the project of psychoanalysis was offered as a means to cure the neurosis either of the teacher or of the student. (33)

Two additional variations bring us closer to the present. In one, represented by such disparate figures as Lacanian child analyst Maud Mannoni and American ego psychologist Erik Erikson, the differences between psychoanalysis and education "were highlighted by attention to culture" (33). A fifth dynamic comes into view "when the project of psychoanalysis began to focus on questions of creativity in education and in psychic elaborations" (33). Britzman calls this fifth movement "the arts of getting by," a formulation that emphasizes the ordinary work of crafting a self capable of tolerating difficulty and of dreaming a future that does not endlessly repeat the conflicts of the past. The regenerative state of "psychic sleeping" that I allude to at the opening of this chapter belongs here, and it marks a new emphasis in thinking about the psychoanalytic setting as especially suited to helping develop unconscious capabilities on the part of both participants (Bollas 2002, 14). Resistance, when it comes to this kind of work, has less to do with the *content* of intolerable ideas and more to do with permitting onself to listen for and follow the queer and apparently nonsensical lines of thought the mind presents.

Although Britzman's study of these dynamics and the individuals associated with them began with what she calls her romantic question of why education cannot "tolerate psychoanalysis" (29), her research takes her to the knot hinted at by Freud: "Both for psychoanalysis and education, there is something deeply disturbing about psychoanalytic theories of learning (which are indistinguishable from theories of the self)" (30). Where Felman finds conflict between psychoanalysis and education, Britzman follows her own question to a surprising conclusion:

> But my question, like all beginning romances, ignored the antinomy within each field, and how the arguments within returned to structure the arguments between them. If either field is offered as a "cure" one loses the elusiveness of the subject in question. One loses the question. (29)

If we approach the knot at the center of relations between psychoanalysis and education from Britzman's perspective, the third term that illuminates the difficult relations is the conflicted and creative process of learning. When we approach the question from Felman's perspective, pedagogy becomes the third term. Indeed, this knot might more fruitfully be thought of as a stubborn tension both between teaching and learning and within each term itself. Freud was no stranger to this tension. Paul Verhaeghe points out that a key development in psychoanalysis occurs at the moment Freud is forced to abandon "the first therapeutic solution proposed by him [which] consists of providing what he considers to be the right knowledge" (2001, 36). Even today, it is not uncommon for psychoanalysts, in discussions about the therapeutic context, to identify teaching with the breakdown in psychoanalytic technique (Laplanche 1999, 228). My own history of learning is marked by a shift from a preoccupation with pedagogy as a meditation on conditions of learning to a preoccupation with learning as a meditation on breakdowns in narratives of learning. I return to Felman's approach to exploring psychoanalysis and education that escapes reductionism and her related interest in the question of implication:

> Reckoning not just with the pedagogical thematics in psychoanalysis but with the pedagogical rhetoric of psychoanalysis, not just with what psychoanalysis says about teachers but with psychoanalysis itself as teacher. (75)

In what way is the clinical experience of psychoanalysis pedagogical? Felman argues that a psychoanalytic education—that is, learning in the context of psychoanalytic treatment and even learning from the study of psychoanalytic theory—does not, indeed must not, proceed from the transmission of the analyst's superior knowledge to the analysand. Now this is a feature that resonates with and is even the driving force behind many contemporary and not so contemporary approaches to pedagogy. Felman recalls Plato's *Meno*, which should perhaps alert us to some constitutive difficulties with rejecting transmission as a metaphor for pedagogical relations. A rejection of transmission also underpins an understanding of and hope for pedagogy that, along with psychoanalytic discussions, was formative in my own education.

In the 1980s, pedagogy became a term invested with a particular force in critical pedagogy and cultural studies in education. David Lusted's (1986) introduction to a special issue of *Screen Education* (then *Screen*) was frequently cited (see, for example, Britzman 1991; Lather 1991; Simon 1992) for his definition of pedagogy, a term Lusted admitted was generally thought to be awkward and elitist, in the service of revitalizing the democratic aims of education. In fact, Lusted's turn to pedagogy was intended to solve two interrelated problems:

> Pedagogy is desperately under-theorized....The problem is that what the concept addresses is crucial and the absence of its development has had material effects. One effect is a share in the failure to realize post-war aspirations towards a genuinely democratic and popular mandatory education system. Another effect is yet another failure; this time to connect radical cultural theory to popular movements whose interest it declares it represents. (3)

This double move considers pedagogy within the realm of school life, but it also poses a challenge to theory, in particular, theory that examines popular culture. Lusted, also hoping to intervene in transmission models of education, wonders "how adequate the theorization of film, TV, culture in general can be without a consciousness of the conditions which produce, negotiate, transform, realize it in practice"(3). A definition of pedagogy follows:

> What pedagogy addresses is the process of production and exchange in this cycle, the transformation of consciousness that takes place in the intersection of three agencies—the teacher, the learner and the knowledge they together produce. If this is to describe a model of relations set by the terms of the social relations of the classroom, it holds good too...in the realm of theory production with the teacher rendered as theorist/critic, the learner as reader/activist and the knowledge as theory. (3)

Lusted's alternative to a model of transmission brings together, under the auspices of media studies, several elements to fire the imagination of educators and educational theorists invested in social change and various struggles against oppression. First, it provides a strong and contemporary language for conceptualizing pedagogy as a relation, not as a linear flow from teacher to student. Second, it considers knowledge as produced in the activities of interaction between texts and learners and among learners, not as a product to be exchanged. Third, it insists upon the responsibility of those involved in cultural production to anticipate and create viable entry points for learners. Finally, it draws attention to the potential of these activities to transform the *consciousness* of learners, a group now conceived to include teachers, students, and theorists working towards more equitable social relations. Consciousness, by the way, refers here to the capacity to make a relationship between what one knows and how one acts in the world. Lusted's definition, in its own way, calls up the three dynamics of implication discussed above. Teachers and students alike learn how their sense of self and desire are organized and addressed by cultural representations; they also learn how social relations of power address some bodies differently than other bodies; finally, the knowledge produced mobilizes an interest in action within and beyond the classroom. Transmission of knowledge, which can only be knowledge that takes for granted and, hence, reproduces existing power relations, is subverted by the insistence that knowledge emerges from the teacher/student/curriculum interactions as they investigate the structures and the structure of appeal of dominant representations.

From Plato to Felman to Lusted, by way of commitments to democracy, individual freedom from oppression, and the capacity to resist complicity in the oppression of others, critical theories of education have identified transmission models of education as the well-spring of the problem. Does psychoanalytic knowledge suggest ways of understanding teaching and learning that illuminate the persistence with which transmission returns to the scene of critical perspectives on education? The knot that Freud finds at the core of relations between psychoanalysis and education suggests that there may be good reasons both for transmission's return and attempts to subvert its force. On the side of guarded optimism, we can observe that transmission models fail to perform as promised or intended. Psychoanalysis offers us a theory of the subject and a theory of learning that undermine the practical effectiveness of transmission as an educational plan while also suggesting something about the anxiety that accompanies helplessness and that returns as rescue fantasies (Britzman 1998; Anna Freud 1974). Psychoanalysis is very interested in several interconnecting phenomena: the establishment and subsequent fragility of the boundary between self and other; the difficulty of determining what comes from the outside of the individual and what comes from internal excitations; the distinction between fantasy and reality; and the emergence of the unconscious as an effect of repression. How we become susceptible to knowledge, how we make sense of the claims knowledge and teachers make upon our sense of self, and how we transform ourselves in our encounters with knowledge and those who represent it constitute questions that destabilize the illusion of unity, at the level of both individual subject and knowledge itself.

Whereas for Lusted the problem of transmission is a conscious dilemma, transmission also reappears on the scene of education to insist upon a different kind of efficiency, one that does not obey the laws of rational thought or communication but rather intrudes upon and disrupts them. This is transference, a term that, in its most ordinary sense, is similar to transmission. There is nevertheless a significant difference between them. The root of transmit means "to send," while the root of transfer means "to bear or carry." The concept of transference, then, comes closer to the dynamics of implication discussed above. Britzman (1998) reminds us of transference's place at the center of *both* education and psychoanalysis:

> In the early relations between education and psychoanalysis, analysts in and close to Freud's circle argued that the dynamical qualities of each field were indistinguishable. This is because psychoanalysis has centred two relations that structure the earliest forms of object relations in learning: those of love and those of authority. Freud made a name for the exchange of love and authority for learning: transference. Transference is perhaps the most central dynamic of time and space that organizes and stalls the practices of learning. The compromised and condensed time of transference catches the "then and there" of the past and the "here and now" of the present. *As a mode of address, the message is derivative of something else, reminiscent of another scene but uncanny in its present urgency.* (33, emphasis added)

These competing pulls of transmission, simultaneously toward its failure or impossibility and toward its inevitability, as transference, are entangled in my own history of learning from psychoanalysis and education in two ways. First, my intellectual biography has been affected by this underground current of transmission as both failure and efficacy. Second, how I think about practice, theory, and research in education has been transformed by the study of psychoanalytic concepts. These strands of influence are neither easily separated into two distinct narratives nor combined into a seamless whole. If education, that is, the history of one's becoming a subject of history, is an effect of the simultaneous impossibility and inevitability of transmission that is not under anyone's control, then we find ourselves with an obligation to rethink, not only what it means to launch a critique of education where transmission is suspected but also what it is that narratives of learning and not learning teach us about how we make sense of the struggle between being affected and defending against being affected. Here, then, in the ways transference interrupts both positive and negative, or, if you will, conservative and progressive notions of transmission, we find one orientation to the paradox of pedagogy and Freud's knot, that particular and peculiar tension between excessive and necessary repression. Let us turn now to a more concrete story of my learning that is marked by and troubles Lusted's definition of pedagogy

Roger Simon was my dissertation supervisor and a very significant figure for a group of students in a graduate program entitled "Critical Pedagogy and Cultural Studies." He wrote an essay for a 1993 conference organized by Jane Gallop. The conference was called "Pedagogy: The Question of the Personal," but, in acknowledgment of a theme that emerged in the conference, the collection was published under a different title: *Pedagogy: The Question of Impersonation* (Gallop 1995a).[3] In returning to Simon's contribution, I am not interested in discovering the teacher's use (or abuse) of the student in spite of or as an effect of his efforts to enact his pedagogical position on teaching and learning which he describes as a mutual relation that affects everyone involved. In this essay, Simon seeks to make visible the conditions of learning that he tries to create as well as some of the obstacles he has encountered in his pedagogical work. I have read the essay several times but focus here on two experiences, the first when the paper was in draft form just prior to the conference. This reading reconstructs the time of not learning. A second reading, which will not be discussed here, tolerates the discovery of my own intellectual desire in the structure of Simon's argument. A few years after completing my dissertation, I came to see more clearly a strong connection between the conceptual framework of my study and this essay of Simon's. Such a reading reconstructs the time of learning as belated, lagging behind doing something with knowledge. Finally, in preparation for this chapter, I consider the first time of reading in relation to Lusted's definition of pedagogy and the tensions between transmission and transference. In this reading, missed meaning subverts Lusted's ideal of pedagogy by insisting upon the difference between the teacher's and the student's times and qualities of learning.

The published version of Simon's essay calls attention to, without resolving, a gap where Lusted places knowledge. Inserted into the essay is a description of some of the comments offered by individuals, including myself, to the essay in its earlier form. Simon hints at this gap when he points out that many of the "cautions and objections" were not particularly helpful to his efforts of moving the paper along. The essay describes the circulation and inhibition of desire between teachers and students. I suspect I was among those worried about the effects of "introducing the notion of erotics and desire into a discussion of pedagogy" (95). Simon reports that "[s]ome thought the word 'desire' too overdetermined with connotations of sexuality, suggesting instead such concepts as affinity, preference, or expectation" (95).

Others worried that the term might be seen as excusing sexual harassment. These concerns can be read as negation (see Chapter Two), which, in psychical terms, allows a repressed idea to be spoken but not accepted. In particular, these responses come close to what Freud called "rejection, by projection, of an idea that has just come up" (1925, 235). Our thoughts may have looked like this: "Of course *you* do not think of desire in these problematic ways, but others might think you do and miss what you have to say." Here we meet a different sense of missed meaning where we worry that others will ruin what we are trying to say. Simon's suggestion that such responses were not helpful reminds us all too clearly of the effects of rejection by projection. Negation is a way of marking missed meaning.

The essay describes Simon's efforts to transgress the legacy of proscription against Jewish "categorical distinctiveness" in relation to his understanding of pedagogy as a form of cultural politics of pedagogy. It provides a rich account of the particular density of the dynamics between doctoral students and their supervisors. Before moving to the specificity of what it means to Simon and to those he encounters that his Jewish identity is implicated in his teaching, he sketches the context—both given and created—of his teaching and my learning:

> At [The Ontario Institute for Studies in Education] 60 percent of the doctoral students are over the age of thirty-five, and approximately 70 percent of the students are women. Most are returning to school after a period of paid employment or unpaid work in the home. They hope a doctoral degree will not only deepen their understanding of issues that are important to them but will also provide the opportunity for an academic career. In this context, they are not only developing a sophisticated analytic ability, but many must confront and rearticulate their personal identities and commitments. Thus, for many students, graduate study can become a time of personal transition, a time of displacement and contradiction when one may become unintelligible to oneself. (97)

Simon takes great care not to rush to restore students' temporary loss of self-intelligibility. Following Felman, he views the loss of intelligibility as a condition for learning from encounters with "readings and discussion intended to probe understanding, interrogate assumptions, and explore the very conditions of learning" (97). Simon called his essay "Face to Face with Alterity: Postmodern Jewish Identity and the Eros of Pedagogy," a title that I read as signalling two dynamics simultaneously. First, Simon investigates the difference identity makes when identity is conceived less as ontology and more as a project. In addition, Simon distinguishes between a form of the teacher's eros that makes its pleasure from evidence of a repetition of the teacher's desire in the student (this would be a fantasy of transmission) and an eros that refuses to satisfy that desire, whether emanating from the teacher or the student. Echoes of Lusted can be detected in his insistence that this difference becomes articulated in the choice to use the teacher's desire "in pedagogical exchange that enhances both student and teacher learning" (100). Yet, in Simon's description of the stakes of learning he values, we discern a hesitation in his acknowledgment of times when, in fact, learning is experienced by students as interference. "The return of difference," he writes, "is not always appreciated, as it may frustrate student desires and lead to a de-eroticization of a faculty image-text" (100). The production of new knowledge on the part of students is deferred. Our unhelpful comments constitute the text of deferred meaning.

Simon draws upon Felman's discussion of Lacanian understandings of the role of the psychoanalyst as necessarily refusing to give the analysand what she wants or thinks she wants in order to force into articulation her own desire. This is the dissolution of the illusion of the subject-supposed-to-know. Simon's pedagogy takes its cue from both Lusted, with an emphasis on knowledge as an effect of pedagogical relations and not its motor, and from Felman's reading of Lacan, with its emphasis on the eroticization of the subject-supposed-to-know. Here is how he describes the dynamics of student investment in faculty:

> The substance of the eroticization of pedagogy of faculty is, in part, articulated in Shoshana Felman's groundbreaking work on the importance of Lacan's theoretical writing for questions of pedagogy, through which one might posit a dimension of a student's desire for a professor as a demand for "the subject-supposed-to-know." Faculty image texts that promise a response to this desire quite sensibly become a locus of attraction. This attraction is doubled if the student believes that recognition by a professor embodying valued image-text characteristics would serve to confer on that student a degree of academic credibility, authorizing his or her "right" to a position in a particular graduate program. (99)

If certain qualities enhance a particular image-text for particular students, hence increasing the investment of eroticization, other qualities can diminish or block such investment. Simon speculates on the ways in which "teaching as a Jew" can produce a de-eroticized image-text for some students. Transmission is subverted by Simon's meditations on his pedagogical commitments; yet, in my view, it returns as transference by the introduction of the subject-supposed-to-know. Such a subject is neither made nor unmade solely by virtue of being in possession of institutional power or scholarly reputation. Rather, the subject-supposed-to-know comes into being when he or she can productively be invested with the love and authority made from one's earliest ties with one's parents. Simon argues that "the complex circuit of signification and eros that conditions the work of teaching and learning...

incorporates but is not fully accounted for by classical notions of transference and counter-transference" (95).

I do not know exactly what he means by "classical," but I understand Lacan's notion of the subject-supposed-to-know to be an effect of transference, that is, someone who comes to be seen as the source of meaning and desire for the analysand. This is precisely what makes its knowledge so desirable and so illusory. The only knowledge that is important, in the analytic setting, is the analysand's knowledge of her own unconscious processes, but this is also the knowledge that is resisted. Bruce Fink (1996) describes how such resistance emerges as a relation to the work of the analyst:

> (...) the analysand, who is perhaps paying attention to manifestations of the unconscious for the first time, *tends to view the analyst as the representative agent of every such manifestation.* The analysand does not take such manifestations upon him- or herself, but instead refuses responsibility for them....*The subject supposed to know—that is, the unconscious "within" the analysand—is rejected by the analysand and projected onto the analyst.* The analyst must agree to occupy the space of or stand in (or sit in) for the unconscious—to make the unconscious present through his or her presence. (31, emphasis in original)

Fink's more clinical discussion of Lacan's subject-supposed-to-know suggests that this is a very tricky notion indeed to draw into the pedagogical context. The frustrating "return of difference" that Simon argues comes from his acting upon what he takes to be his Jewish specificity is not of the same order as the analyst's return to the analysand the difference of her own unconscious knowledge. Our responses to his paper, on the one hand, do enact a refusal of Simon's difference, but I think some uncertainty remains as to the content of our refusal which, you will recall, expresses itself as an anxiety about the naming of eros as a presence in our relations with our teacher. Such anxiety suggests a heightened erotic investment, albeit unconscious, rather than its withdrawal.

Simon's project fleshes out some socio-historical dimensions of teacher/student relations and in so doing makes a significant contribution to our thinking about what is at stake in how we attach and do not attach to knowledge and those who represent knowledge. The undigested and, indeed, indigestible responses to his draft suggest, however, that the conflicted experience of transference interferes with, even as it animates, learning in surprising ways. Indeed, to return to a question I posed early on in this chapter: how do we tell the difference between a leap away from and a leap toward learning? We can now respond through a new way of thinking about learning as necessarily wavering between application and implication, as made from the discarded material of missed meaning and negation, and, finally, as reconstructed rather than reported.

These dynamics repeat in educational research, and, so, one final move is in order. Interpretation in educational research does not settle meaning. Not only is it marked by its own inherent missed meaning and negation, educational research, like theory, also generates missed meaning and negation in those who encounter its narratives. Implicating the doctrines, that puzzling formulation of Felman's, does offer a method for crafting an autobiography of learning when taken through the development of psychoanalysis where the learner notices how she reads; how she has been affected by encounters with knowledge and those who represent it; and how the untangling of prior attachments produces new entanglements. Autobiography, then, might be thought of as a laboratory where the narrator's educational experience of leaping away from and leaping toward learning is worked through. This is the time of *Nacherziehung* or after-education that also belongs to the force of education.

Notes

1. I am not alone in my ambivalence. Without resorting to a nostalgia for the autonomous subject of humanism, Deanne Bogdan (1992) considers the limits of discourse theory in relation to reading literature by making a distinction between literary experience, that is, "textual engagement in terms of the direct or participating response to literature" and literary literacy or the "awareness of as many as possible of the conditions of that experience" (xxx). Nancy Chodorow (1999) argues that a theory of meaning must account for both social construction and personal creation: "Meaning is an inextricable mixture of the sociocultural and historically contextualized on the one hand and the personally psychodynamic and psychobiographically contexualized on the other" (2).

2. My thanks to Susanne Luhman, who, in her native language, puzzled over this text with me.

3. This conference and the published work that followed turned out to be central to my own work in ways that only became visible as I was compiling this manuscript. Not only was the conference significant in terms of the scholarship it provoked on questions of the personal in education, it also became an event where student protest over what some students saw as Gallop's pedagogical failure suggested difficulties and complexities that spilled out over the margins of scheduled participation. I return to this narrative in Chapter Seven.

Chapter Two

Fantasizing Women in the Women's Studies Classroom: Toward a Symptomatic Reading of Negation

"Lesbians are not women." So concludes Monique Wittig (1980) in the "The Straight Mind," an essay that reached English-speaking audiences in 1978. This terse sentence is amplified in a footnote that reads, "No more is any woman who is not in a relation of personal dependency with a man"(111). Along with Wittig's "One Is Not Born a Woman"(1981), this essay identifies the heterosexual contract and its systems of thought and economic relations as the productive and reproductive center of all relations of subordination and domination, not only those that exist between men and women. Wittig's argument focuses on the material effects of language. It reconfigures a question that has been and continues to be central to feminist theoretical debate. For Wittig, to ask, "What is woman?" is already to remain within the conceptual confines of heterosexual imperatives. To continue to speak of "woman" or even "women" will not effect the political, economic, or ideological transformations envisioned by feminisms precisely because these concepts are irredeemably saturated by, even as they saturate, what she calls "the straight mind."

Although Wittig is quite adamant that, by virtue of their social practices, lesbians neither love nor are women, her little footnote of "no more" refuses ontological claims as the basis for resistance against oppression. For Wittig, lesbian must be thought of as a political category strategically poised to potentially include any woman "who is not in a relation of personal dependency with a man." This, of course, leads to different definitional problems: What is a lesbian? Can there be heterosexual relations that refuse the terms of the heterosexual contract? Does a woman's desire to alter her conditions of dependency qualify her to identify herself with the political category of lesbian?

From the perspective of much contemporary feminist theorizing, the resonance of these questions seems tied to the ethos and preoccupations of the radical feminisms of the late 1970s. While it has become commonplace to work the categories "women" and "men" as political, historical, and social identities complicated by race, class, and sex, Wittig's dream of a world without "women" seems odd, if not downright chauvinistic. This is particularly the case in Women's Studies, where female students' capacity to recognize themselves as women within the terms of the course is a significant measure both of the course's success and of students' success in the course. But even in Women's Studies' classrooms, where ongoing pedagogical attempts to challenge commonsense notions of what it means to be a woman, the figure of the lesbian continues to be a disturbing, perhaps even uncanny, presence.[1]

Freud's (1919b) notion of the uncanny (*die Unheimlich*) signals something that is familiar but strangely so. He describes the uncanny as a particular quality of feeling provoked when an event or image unsettles a foundational certainty and returns the individual momentarily to the vulnerability of individual or collective infancy. In his words,

> (...) an uncanny experience occurs either when infantile complexes which have been repressed are once more revived by some impression, or when primitive beliefs which have been surmounted seem once more to be confirmed. (249)

The notion of the uncanny disrupts the dream of learning as a developmental progression through the fantasy of what Madeline Grumet (1989) has termed "the beautiful curriculum." It also draws attention to the work of fantasy in individuals' attempts to figure out how knowledge, staged as curriculum, might be relevant to them. In Women's Studies' classrooms, this process turns centrally on the extent to which students perceive that their feminist teachers and the texts that represent women from feminist perspectives tell the truth about their own lives and sense of self. At the level of the everyday, one may not think very much about the categories of men, women, and children, even as one has no (apparent) difficulty in locating oneself within these categories. However, in Women's Studies classes, these positions are viewed as social constructions that are organized by larger social relations of power. In these classes, sociological notions of positionality in relation to women's civil rights and struggles for equality are offered in order to provide women with new ways to interpret their experiences and struggle for better futures. Just beginning to be explored (Felman 1993; Finke 1993; Gallop 1995b) is the question of how these new interpretations are lived at the level of the psyche where difference refers, not to social differences between individuals but to differences within individuals. The pedagogical problem, I will be arguing, is that much of the work of making a relation to knowledge takes place in the unconscious, where fantasmatic ideals anchor the sense of the self as cohesive and coherent (Phelan 1993; Silverman

1996). This is the psychic work of identification, and its processes may be implicated in, but not subsumed by, social relations of domination and subordination.

Indeed, a recurring theme in recent educational research that investigates student learning about social difference is the persistence of a gap between the transformatory hopes, articulated within pedagogical strategies, and curricular scores and their apparent effects on students (Bogdan 1994; Britzman 1992; Ellsworth 1989; Ladson-Billings 1996; Lather 1991). This theme takes shape in two directions identifying, on the one hand, some learners' refusals to understand the perspectives of *other* socially marginalized identities as having anything to do with them. On the other hand, several researchers have become concerned when counter-hegemonic knowledge may be perceived as telling the "truth," but the immediate effects of this new knowledge seem more debilitating rather than transformatory. What these two kinds of observations share is a concern with what knowledge does to people. They suggest that theorizing curriculum and pedagogy might benefit from understanding learning as a psychic event that involves the realms of both conscious and unconscious operations.

This essay considers what such understanding entails by exploring disturbances to one woman's imagined relation to femininity. What is at stake in this story, however, is not so much our capacity to *read* the psychic difficulties individuals experience in their encounters with knowledge, an issue I explore in greater detail below. The kind of study I am proposing may help critical educators to re-examine our own assumptions and expectations about what we imagine students are up to when they speak (or not) and write (or not) in our classrooms. I develop this general claim by focusing on the specific context of an introductory Women's Studies course. When we consider psychic dimensions of learning in relation to some persistent dilemmas within the feminist education, new questions emerge about the curious relationships among the (re)presentation of identities as curriculum, teachers' investments in the curriculum, and the nature of the work of learning. These dilemmas have to do with the organization of feminist curriculum within an epistemological framework that, on the one hand, privileges gender as its primary analytical category and, on the other hand, collapses the meaning of categories of social difference with and within North American feminism's own anxious history of exclusions and marginalizations.

I begin with a sketch of Wittig's polemic because the conclusion ("Lesbians are not women") of her theoretical argument works against the habit within much North American feminist education to include lesbians within the category of women. Within the dominant narrative, lesbians share gender identity with heterosexual women, and lesbians are oppressed both as women and as lesbians. What this narrative cannot admit is that gender identity may always be lived in very complicated ways in relation to normative (heterosexual) femininity. Wittig can be read as implying that normative femininity is a precarious construct that must be continually (re)enforced and that sometimes fails. Her essay can be taken as a comment on identity formation as that which can exceed such normativity.[2] Put somewhat differently, we could say that, for Wittig, the lesbian is a character in a theoretical work of fiction that holds new possibilities for how feminists might imagine and alter their social and psychic landscapes. In a more broadly conceived gesture, we could say that all representations present characters in theoretical works of fiction, and we might be surprised at the range of uses—at the level of fantasy—a reader may make of a character.

Notes on Methodology

Using excerpts from one woman's story of her participation in an introductory Women's Studies course, I examine the relationship she articulates between her self-understandings as a woman and the relevant subject positions—woman, feminist, lesbian—articulated by the course curriculum. I focus on the ways in which this relationship can be seen as relying upon, even as it is bothered by, the place within the course of the figure of the lesbian. The reading I offer of this student's response to lesbianism begins with two assumptions. The first assumption concerns what it means to bring individuals' narratives into our research stories. Just as *the lesbian* is a character in Wittig's theoretical fiction, the *real* student, who describes her encounter with feminist knowledge, is also a character in her own story. This is so, in part, because, as Linda Brodkey (1987) insists, narratives about experience must not be collapsed with experience itself. When it comes to interpreting narratives told to us in the context of research, the insights of poststructuralism meet the insights of psychoanalytic theory to compound the impossible dream of representation. As Roy Schafer (1983), a psychoanalyst who theorizes narration itself as experience, argues:

> We are forever telling stories about ourselves. In telling these stories to others we may… be said to perform straightforward narrative actions. In saying that we tell them to ourselves, however, we are enclosing one story within another….On this view, the self is a telling. (218)

If the stories we tell to others are also stories we tell to ourselves, we might ask how these stories work to enhance our image of our identity as cohesive and coherent. By asking this question of the stories told as stories about classroom experiences, we can become curious about the stories as having to do with the encounter between how one represents the self to the self (and others) and how classroom experiences organize and disorganize these self-representations. Thus, I read this student's narrative for the struggles it reveals between common sense understandings of what it means to be a woman and feminist understandings. I further argue that her response to lesbianism can be read as symptomatic of a conflict inherent in much feminist education.

The conflict turns on the theoretical and pedagogical difficulties of retaining "women" as a unified political category while simultaneously dispersing the category to include feminist discourses' historically excluded others. When we say that students who refuse to recognize themselves in relation to these new terms *resist* our pedagogical efforts, we may be foreclosing opportunities to gain insight into the work of theorizing identity that these students, however problematically, undertake. One of the purposes of this chapter is to consider what it means to interpret the work of resistance on the part of learners as the work of identification. Towards the end of the chapter, I return to the conflict named above and the questions it provokes for theorizing pedagogy and curriculum.

My interpretive strategy of reading a student's engagement with a particular curricular staging of feminist knowledge as symptomatic of a conflict embedded within the staging itself can be compared with Gallop's (1992) method of "symptomatic reading" in *Around 1981: Academic Feminist Literary Theory.* She describes "symptomatic reading" as coming "out of psychoanalytic method by way of deconstruction" (7), and she distinguishes her approach from that of new criticism:

> Where new critical close reading embraces the text in order to more fully and deeply understand its excellences, "symptomatic reading" squeezes the text tight to force it to reveal its perversities. New criticism is appreciative, even worshipful; symptomatic reading tends to be demystifying, even aggressive. (7)

Perhaps acts of demystification are necessarily aggressive insofar as they uncover something preferably left alone, something that, in psychoanalytic terms, is repressed from conscious apprehension. Like Gallop, I am interested in what psychoanalytic theory offers to our understanding of the dynamics embedded within social and political events. I bring this interest to my study of classroom events—the organization and selection of knowledge as curriculum and the attachments and refusals enacted in pedagogical encounters. Gallop's method of symptomatic reading is useful because it asks all of us to consider our implication in an intellectual and political history that has been formative to what and how we teach and, more importantly, what and how we learn.

For Gallop, the feminist critical anthologies used in Women's Studies "are good places to witness the dynamics of collectivity" (7). She proposes reading anthologies as a whole, but what she attends to may be unfamiliar to feminist readers whose epistemological attachments are structured by humanistic notions of identity and experience. She offers the following description of her goals:

> The necessary assumption...is that we are all inevitably symptomatic, we are all subjects and thus speak from within a field of conflict. It is not my goal to unveil the inadequacies of any individual. Reading an anthology as a whole is a method for getting at "symptoms" which recur across various authors. Rather than pointing to some individual's blind spots, these might indicate conflicts inhering in a collective situation. I am interested in the marks produced in the discourse of knowledge by a subject, not by an individual but by a collective subject, the academic feminist critic. (7)

The period Gallop addresses in her study (1972–1982) also produced important writing, including several anthologies (Bowles and Klein 1983; Bunch and Pollack 1983; Culley and Portuges 1985), about feminist classrooms and pedagogical practices. Rather than squeeze these texts, I want to bring the notion of symptomatic reading to bear on a set of relations that are performed in the feminist classroom. We might think of the text of pedagogy as the story of a collective situation that brings together not only actors (teachers, students, and texts) but also dynamics (investments, interpretations, desires) that are historically situated and conflicted in very particular and complex ways. Reading such a text as a whole means that we attend not only to the curriculum and what it includes or leaves out. Nor does the kind of reading Gallop proposes lend insight into the supposed relations between our pedagogical efforts and the student's success or failure. Moving backward and forward, the stakes of a symptomatic reading consider the tensions between two sites of interpretation to reveal the structures of their investment. One site concerns teachers' responses to students' engagement with the curriculum; a second site concerns students' claims about their engagement.

Gallop's notion of symptomatic reading is useful because it distinguishes between texts, including the text of research data and the individuals who produce these texts.[3] That is, by arguing that we are all symptomatic, Gallop insists that we attend to the ways in which we speak through the conflicts and contradictions inherent in a time and place even as these conflicts speak through us. Gallop's symptomatic readings of the essays produced by people she considers to be her peers and colleagues are different from my symptomatic reading of one student's story and the curriculum she engages, in that Gallop takes up the terms of a debate about how a field of knowledge production is to be defined. My own readings, however, insert a different sense of time into the equation. This is the messy time of learning where the histories of students meet the histories of the teacher. Two central questions inform this chapter. One question asks what we can learn about our own (collective) pedagogical assumptions, intellectual histories and investments when we study our students' stories of engagement. The second question asks what these stories of engagement can teach us about the detours of learning. I turn now to my version of one student's engagement with feminist knowledge.

Stories of Representation: Where the Fictional Self Meets Its Fictional Other

Lynne Hunt, a white woman in her late thirties, volunteered to participate in my study of student engagement in an introductory Women's Studies' course (Pitt 1995). At the time of the course, she was in the process of making a life for herself that did not center around her responsibilities as a wife and mother. However, the changes in her life were not ones she had engineered. She was responding to the significance of structural changes brought on by the acrimonious break-up of her marriage due, to some extent, to her attempts within the marriage to exceed her roles as wife and mother. She recognized that her story was a familiar one to feminists. Still, she left the course unconvinced that feminism served her needs.

Lynne was uncomfortable with what she perceived to be a demand of the class that she both tell her story and listen to the stories of others. This constitutes one set of refusals on Lynne's part to recognize herself within the sites of identification that were offered by the course. More pertinent to my concerns here, however, is Lynne's refusal to recognize lesbians as women and to consider discussions about lesbian sexuality as a relevant topic for a Women's Studies course. At first glance, her response seems to resonate with Bonnie Zimmerman's (1985) claim that "heterosexuals often have difficulty accepting that a lesbian, especially a role-playing 'butch', is in fact a woman" (203). This American feminist critic *knows* that lesbians are women just as Wittig *knows* they are not. But what, in fact, does Lynne know, and why, in my engagements with Lynne, did the topic of lesbianism dominate our discussions about the course?

According to Lynne, silence fell over the class when one instructor declared her lesbian identity and when she then asked students to think about what lack of mainstream representation meant for her day-to-day life and the class's capacity to know about lesbians. For Lynne, the group's silence confirmed her view that lesbianism was an issue that did not belong in Women's Studies. But before considering Lynne's (mis)understanding of this event, what did the teacher want? This is the first turn of the teacher's implication in a structure of desire that overdetermines how students' responses can be read.

When representation is presumed to do the pedagogical work of affirming minority identities and persuading others of the intolerable conditions of their everyday life, two narrow sites of identification are offered. One site of identification this teacher offered was addressed to students who are lesbians. But this desire to be a role model may not work, for there are significant differences among lesbians. The other site of identification is addressed to students who do not recognize themselves as lesbians. There, two positions are offered that are complicitous. Students can either agree or disagree that the lesbian, as a woman, is doubly oppressed, first as a woman and second as a "sexual deviant." If they disagree, their response is still complicitous because it occupies (negatively) one of the positions implied in the structure of the demand. It may be complicitous in a second way as well, and this has to do with the ways in which these (negative) responses affirm the teacher's assumptions about students as homophobic.

Lynne's response complicates the two positions offered that require her to either accept or refuse to accept the view that patriarchal social systems place a double burden of oppression on lesbians. As we shall see, her response to the introduction of "lesbianism as an issue" and to the teacher's offering of herself as "a representative lesbian" is quite curious because Lynne agrees that lesbians should be granted civil rights. But she refuses to understand this political struggle as relevant to Women's Studies. For Lynne, lesbian oppression is not a "women's issue." Her refusal, akin to the structure of disavowal, where one simultaneously recognizes and ignores a traumatic perception, is central to structuring her understanding of the course and of feminism. What is surprising (and instructive) about Lynne's story is that the meanings she attaches to the figure of the lesbian, which she returns to the real lesbian teacher, bother her sense of herself as in control of her identity. This desire for self-control is already complicated by what Lynne believes to be the pedagogical demand that lies at the center of the course: the demand to identify with women as victims of oppression. Is it possible to understand Lynne's refusal to identify as a victim as continuous with her refusal to identify lesbians as women? If these two refusals are continuous, how does this alter or complicate an interpretation of her response as blatantly homophobic? Let us take a closer look at her response.

Lynne denies the importance of a discussion of lesbianism to feminism and expresses dismay at the time devoted to it (one class of twelve) when topics that seem more important, such as the plight of First Nations women, received what she perceived to be insufficient attention. A conscientious student, Lynne will not even read the assigned material on lesbians. She describes lesbianism as a gay rights issue that has little relevance to Women's Studies and suggests that lesbians have seized opportunistically on Women's Studies because of a shared femaleness. During an interview she said,

> [W]omen who choose that lifestyle have as much right, I suppose, to say, "Well, I'm a lesbian and therefore I'm entitled to be accepted by society. I shouldn't have to sort of hide my lifestyle because I choose this or feel persecution because I've chosen this lifestyle."
>
> [T]his makes this issue viable, but it's not viable if it's "Well, here's an opportunity to bring women and their issues to the surface, and while we're at it, why not get a cause going for lesbianism and therefore if we can get, you know, women to support us on so many issues maybe they'll support us on this too."

The above quote is a contradictory moment in a much longer passage, where Lynne describes lesbianism as not relevant to Women's Studies and implies that lesbians are not women. However, Lynne also recognizes that it is on the basis of "femaleness" that lesbians stake a claim to Women's Studies space. But the above quote identifies three identificatory positions: women, lesbians, and Lynne. Thus she must recast lesbianism as a personal choice that is neither relevant nor important to women's struggles against oppression. Lynne asserts a strong minoritizing view (Sedgwick 1990) of sexuality: lesbians are defined by their object choice and are only relevant to a minor population and have nothing to do with her. Hence, for Lynne, lesbians are irrelevant to Lynne.

But at the same time as Lynne is refusing to know lesbians or know about lesbians, she does engage with the issue; in fact, it becomes the most elaborated topic for us. Her written and verbal engagement with the issue contradicts her stated refusal to know and, following Foucault (1980), can be interpreted as an erotic incitement to discourse on the taboos of sexuality. Foucault describes this as the "speaker's benefit." He writes, "If sex is repressed, that is condemned to prohibition, then the mere fact that one is speaking about it has the appearance of a deliberate transgression" (6). But this is no simple transgression as it plays itself out through the barriers of repression. Foucault is referring not only to one's own confessional talk about sexuality but to an entire culture's fascination with it. This is even more complex within Women's Studies. There minoritizing understandings about sexuality—that sexuality originates in the self—clash with feminist attempts to address the colonization of women's sexuality by men and the exclusion and marginalization of lesbians within feminist discourses.

For Lynne, lesbianism exceeds the bounds of what she will identify as a women's issue—lesbians are oppressed because they are lesbians, not because they are women. At the same time, her preoccupation with a very minor part of the course is an indication of the significance that it holds for her. The lesbian, whether she is figured in terms of woman-identification or in terms of a refusal of (identification against) normative femininity, may suggest to Lynne the precariousness of her own ability to present herself as a woman, already presumed heterosexual, to assert itself as natural and originary. The problem is that Lynne understands her identity as always already there, and what she cannot tolerate is the idea, central to psychoanalytic theories of the subject, of the subject who is not in mastery of herself. As we shall see below, the figure of the lesbian destabilizes Lynne's belief in her identity, and it does so in two different ways. The first has to do with the similarities between Lynne's identificatory position and that which she attributes to lesbians. The second has to do with the collapse among woman-identification, feminism, and lesbian feminism. This is what Katie King (1994) is signalling in her argument that lesbianism came to function as "feminism's magical sign" during the late sixties and early seventies, and it organizes the second turn in much of feminist education's structure of desire.

King argues that the familiar axiom "feminism is the theory, lesbianism is the practice" was deployed in "a historical context in which lesbianism and feminism are not automatically assumed to be necessarily overlapping categories, and in which the phrase is being newly evolved in the women's movement to privilege lesbianism" (125). Apparently, however, in her 1970 talk to the New York Chapter of Daughters of Bilitis, Ti-Grace Atkinson, to whom the axiom is attributed, emphasized that lesbians and feminists were different groups, the first requiring civil rights for a small minority and the second naming the grounds for political revolution. Atkinson argued against their political agendas being collapsed when she said, "Feminism is a theory; but lesbianism is a practice" (King, 125).

The difference is significant but not because of the separation presumed between theory and practice. Rather the misquoted but popularized version, instead of allowing a more universalizing discourse of sexuality that could hold onto the tensions *between* sexual desires and practices and political identifications, emerged from and re-installed a minoritizing view. That is, in the terms of Eve Sedgwick's (1990) definition of the homosexual/heterosexual divide, the question of lesbianism for feminism might have become "an issue of continuing, determinative importance in the lives of people across the spectrum of sexualities" (1).

Wittig's argument, referred to at the beginning of this chapter, provides one way of exploring this terrain; Adrienne Rich's (1980) famous essay, "Compulsory Heterosexuality and Lesbian Existence," provides another. However, as the concept of gender developed into the analytic category that could encompass heterosexual women and lesbians in a common struggle against misogyny, what has emerged is a dual claim that is overly reductive of the positions of both Wittig and Rich: all women could be lesbian, and all lesbians could be women. According to King, this poses a new set of problems:

> Identifying with lesbianism falsely implies that one knows all about heterosexism and homophobia magically through identity or association. The "experience" of lesbianism is offered as salvation from the individual practice of heterosexism and homophobia as the source of intuitive institutional and structural understanding of them. The power of lesbianism as a privileged signifier makes analysis of heterosexism and homophobia difficult, since it obscures the need for counter-intuitive challenges to ideology. (136)

Following King's insights, one could say that Lynne's refusal to identify lesbians as relevant to herself breaks the central assumption that visibility ensures representation. Visibility does something for Lynne other than what the teacher ostensibly desires. Indeed, Lynne is preoccupied with the figure of the lesbian, and one might venture to view her refusal as acting much like the *No* in the psychoanalytic dialogue. For Freud (1925, 35), the utterance of a *No* almost always turns out to be a *Yes*. The criticisms he experienced for this resonate with one of the central problems of critical and feminist pedagogical practice. That is, how are we to interpret resistance to knowledge that goes against the grain of common sense if we don't want to get stuck in the rut of false consciousness where the teacher holds the power of superior knowledge? Freud's understanding of negation can help us here.

He argues that the contents of the unconscious, repressed knowledge of the pre-oedipal, are not, strictly speaking, available to consciousness although they *speak* in condensed and distorted forms in dreams, slips of the tongue, etc. But negation provides another route from the unconscious to consciousness. Freud (1925) argues that

> (...) the content of a repressed image or idea can make its way into consciousness, on the condition that it is negated. Negation is a way of taking cognizance of what is repressed, indeed it is already a lifting of the repression, though not, of course, an acceptance of what is repressed. (236)

Through this process of negation a kind of intellectual engagement with what is repressed is achieved, but, at the same time, what is essential to the repression remains preserved, still out of reach in the unconscious. This, after all, is Freud's famous dictum: the return of the repressed. I interpret this to mean that an idea that is negated is associated with repressed content and that, while the negation of an idea permits an airing of the repressed content, the grammatical removal of the negation does not in itself result in an expression of the content of the repressed idea. This is, in fact, not unlike how Lynne understands the function of personal experience in the feminist classroom: the stories are told, but their narration achieves nothing. We will not be further ahead, then, if we merely hear Lynne's statement that lesbianism does not belong on the syllabus as a masked assertion that it is in fact central, or that knowledge designed to contest negative stereotypes will change her mind. We have to understand that the denial stands for, but is not equal to, something that she cannot allow to become registered in consciousness. Essentially, Lynne's refusal of the lesbian may serve as a decoy to her own attempt to maintain and assert a semblance of her identity as cohesive and coherent. The lesbian became a substitute for acknowledging her own contradictory struggles, already provoked, at least in part, by her belief that feminism demanded that she see herself as a victim. Thus one might say that the reason Lynne views the lesbian as beside the point is because the point itself is unbearable.

What lies at the center of my interpretation of how the figure of the lesbian threatens to destabilize Lynne's identity is the contradictory, yet familiar, image of the lesbian as both a man-hater and a man-imitator. The first image shores up Lynne's assertion that feminism has trouble separating itself from man-hating, and the second recalls her own investments in positive identifications with men. She tells two stories about the lesbian instructor as proof that lesbians must be seen outside the project of feminism. In the following interview excerpt, anti-male bias slides onto the lesbian instructor:

> And while in the term papers one cannot be biased against men, there can't be sort of anti-male content in the term papers, in the open discussions there was very much that content in it, and the issue of lesbianism, especially because of (the instructor's) being a lesbian, she was very much anti-male.

This description is part of a story about a classroom incident in which one woman's male partner arrived to view a film about women and pornography. The class had previously voted that this would be permitted, but it was at a time when the other instructor was present. The instructor on this occasion told the young man that the class would have to vote on whether or not he would be permitted to stay. Lynne interpreted this action as unfairly and aggressively singling him out and embarrassing her and the other members of the class:

> I rather thought that singled him out and isn't this what women are trying to change? And we all had to vote and she took an—I thought was aggressive in her manner. It wasn't even a matter of—it wasn't even directed towards him, it was directed towards the rest of us....
>
> There were quite a few women there who weren't shy about speaking up, so I don't think it was a matter of her having to rescue us or anything like that, and actually, most of us felt embarrassed because she had put him in such a position.

In this story, Lynne associates the lesbian teacher with anti-male attitude that she suggests permeates the course. However, this is the only specific incident she refers to, and, in her re-telling of it, she makes the lesbian responsible for anti-male bias even as she separates her from what she perceives to be the proper role of feminism.

In the second story, Lynne associates present-day lesbians with the butches and femmes she observed in her childhood, which she spent in an area of Toronto known even then for its gay population. Her memories focused on the women whose "imitation" of masculinity was articulated through their attire, their voices, their use of "coarse" language, and their mannerisms. As a child she was fascinated by the strangeness of these women, who, along with prostitutes and their clients, made for exotic street scenes, the explanations for which Lynne relied on an older sister-in-law.

When she carries these images forward into the classroom where lesbianism has been accorded a place alongside of what she considers to be more important and relevant issues, she translates the appearance of the fifties butch (apprehended from a distance) into a new form of tyranny over women. The instructor had told students that they could drop their assignments off at her home (not mentioned by Lynne is the fact that this arrangement allowed students more time with their assignments). However, she warned them that they should not come after a certain hour in the evening because her partner would get upset. Lynne concludes from this that women who seek female partners fail in their bid for equality and only repeat the tyranny of heterosexual relationships, a tyranny with which Lynne has first-hand experience. Elsewhere she writes:

> While I do not advocate anti-lesbian rights, I am not willing to join causes to endorse lesbianism as a way of life for myself or my daughters. The bottom line for my lack of clarity on this issue of controversy is that the very reason lesbians exist is because some women have chosen to become pro-female, but in some cases as a retaliation against males. Ironically, even one of the female role adopts the traditional male behaviour, the same behaviour most heterosexual women are committed to eliminating.

In this jumble of contradictory statements, Lynne seems to imply that opportunities to learn about lesbians are little more than thinly veiled recruitment efforts. While lesbians "have chosen to become pro-female," their efforts fail precisely because one partner assumes the male role of oppressor. Lynne understands lesbian relationships in terms that refuse their difference, choosing instead to reinscribe them as a bad imitation of heterosexual and, as such, anti-feminist as well.

There is, however, a caveat in Lynne's refusal: she acknowledges that gay men and lesbians do need to struggle for social equality. Still, she sums up her position in relation to the matter with this statement: "I try to be balanced in my thinking, and I have to say that I would prefer not to know lesbians." But how might knowing lesbians make Lynne lose her balance? We'll take a closer look at what Lynne is refusing below. As we do so, we might want to be mindful that "balancing acts" are already implicated within Women's Studies. These might be characterized as three dimensions of ambivalence that are provoked by Women's Studies but that cannot be resolved there. The first has to do with what one does with the difficult knowledge of women's oppression, male dominance, and the different ways in which these are lived. The second has to do with the awareness that Women's Studies is something of an island, in relation to both the university and the larger social world. Finally, there is the question of what Women's Studies does with the social knowledge that lesbians are suspect just about everywhere but in Women's Studies.

While these ambivalences may constitute the conditions of learning within Women's Studies, they are also pushed aside when Women's Studies relies upon a theory of knowledge that assumes that counter-hegemonic representations transform learners unproblematically. Unaccounted for in this theory of knowledge, which only *appears* to bypass these ambivalences, is the question of how one psychically attaches to new knowledge. Ambivalence, however, returns in encounters with new knowledge because there is something uncanny about knowledge itself. That is, knowledge promises but never quite delivers the truth about the self. In the Women's Studies classroom, the promise that cannot be delivered concerns the truth about gender identity. As we return to Lynne's claim ("I try to be balanced in my thinking, and I have to say that I would prefer not to know lesbians"), we will take a closer look at a psychic drama that is shut out of pedagogical considerations of what knowledge about gender means to individuals. At first glance it may appear that the contours of this drama are particular to Lynne. It is, after all, her narrative that I have centered in my discussion. What I am suggesting, however, is that Lynne's story expresses the impossibility of occupying unambivalently a gendered identity, and that this impossibility is a condition of identity in our culture. While it is the figure of the lesbian that returns Lynne to this uncanny apprehension, it may also be her story that returns Women's Studies to its own uncanny knowledge summed up famously by Denise Riley (1988) when she asks, *am I that name*?

The Uncanny Return of the Ambivalence of Gender

As we have seen, within the terms offered by the course and, indeed, within the now-familiar educational attempts to reduce homophobia in the classroom, Lynne's refusal to see the relevance of lesbian sexuality for feminist struggles can only be read as the familiar homophobic response of a heterosexual woman. This reading functions within the demand that those who occupy the socially dominant positions (heterosexual women) develop the capacity to tolerate and accept lesbian difference. This demand, however inadvertently, may collapse gender identity with sex and sexuality (see Cornell 1992). Now, given that the concept of gender is useful for feminist discourses precisely because many believe that it separates sexual difference from biological difference (de Lauretis 1987), this is a serious problem. What I am suggesting is that replacing sexual difference with gender difference as an analytical tool for "referring to the exclusively social origins of the subjective identities of men and women" (Scott 1986, 1056) continues the tradition of relying upon the categorization of sexed bodies into two. Left unexamined is the logic of heterosexual imperatives that demands a stable separation between masculinity and femininity. Lynne's story muddles this equation and reveals the psychic work of fashioning a sex/gender identity, work that remains concealed within contexts that conceptualize gender and sexuality as stable and as originating within the self. Here I am referring to the curriculum.

The stories Lynne tells about lesbians hold three clues about the psychic dilemmas that she may be attempting to work through via the figure of lesbian. By excluding lesbians from the category of women, Lynne displaces her own ambivalence about membership in that category. This is the first clue, and it echoes Wittig's insistence that women who are not in a relation of dependence on a man require a new conceptual category. By insisting that lesbians hate men, Lynne maintains her own belief that she can wander between the generalities of critique of male oppression of women and the specificities of her own experiences (which she acknowledges as the effects of male domination) without risking outrage at men. In other words, the difficult emotional labor required to maintain a boundary between an attack on sexism and an attack on men is attenuated when lesbians are represented as man-haters. This is the second clue. And, finally, by attributing to lesbians some of what she considers to be male sexist behavior, Lynne's idealization of a positive identification with men remains uncontaminated. That is, and paradoxically so, it is lesbians who are the real men! Taken together these clues serve her representation of herself as a heterosexual woman.

These "clues" require the logic of psychic negation. This is so because, in order to examine and in a sense work through the repetitions required for such a story to cohere, Lynne would have to "self-destruct."[4] What I mean by this is that the identificatory processes that work ongoingly to secure identity also expose identity as always and already threatened by its own failure to assert itself as natural and originary. But the phantasmatic structure of identity that is secured, however provisionally, by the processes of assuming a sexed position bears, as well, an identificatory relation to its own disavowed imperatives. Judith Butler (1993) argues that

> Sexuality is as much motivated by the fantasy of retrieving prohibited objects as by the desire to remain protected from the threat of punishment such a retrieval might bring on. (100)

The normalized positions of the masculine and feminine are configured by the regulatory demands of heterosexual desire and identity. Butler suggests that, whatever other complexities are involved in the ongoing process of performing identity, identification with a sexed position is a double identification. Entailed here is not only the identification with the phantasmatic ideal of the position (which requires identification with the same-sex parent and an identification of the opposite-sex parent as an object choice). What is also entailed is identification with the position's constitutive limit. In the case of the feminine position, according to Butler, this limit is the figure of the castrator, the figure of excessive phallicism who symbolizes *for* the masculine position the threat of castration.

This framework conceptualizes sexual positions as relations, not self-reliant units, and it can help us to better understand Lynne's response to feminism. What is at stake for her is any disruption to the ways in which she has already negotiated her identity as a woman who loves men. This position does not approximate or idealize "ideal femininity," but rather it is one that approximates identification with the "masculine position." It is a position that is invested in both *being*—functioning as the guarantor that the male is not castrated—and *having* the phallus, refusing her status as castrated. What Lynne must disavow is that a position that approximates *having* the phallus cannot be so easily reconciled with the feminine position of *being* it.

Not only is this position prohibited within the symbolic order of patriarchy, but, for different reasons, it seems to be prohibited within feminist discourses as well. Biddy Martin (1994) describes this as "feminists' injunctions to identify with and as women, over and against masculinity" (105). Butler speculates that the abjected figure of the feminine position's constitutive other is symbolically represented by the "phallicized dyke." But in a more broadly conceived gesture, she also argues that the "hierarchized and differential specular relation" between the masculine and the feminine

> (...) is itself established through the exclusion and abjection of a domain of relations in which all the wrong identifications are pursued; men wishing to "be" the phallus for other men; women wishing to "have" the phallus for other women; women wishing to "be" the phallus for other women.... (103)

Lynne's contradictory positionings of the figure of the lesbian and the meanings she attaches to this figure represent the repudiated forms of both of her significant identifications. That is, through her abjection of the lesbian, Lynne repudiates both her status as castrated and her prohibited wish to have the phallus.

Pedagogical Implications

When lesbianism is treated as a category of social difference among women, gender identity is reduced to a fact of biology, and heterosexuality is re-aligned with gender identity. When feminist pedagogy assumes that women's political mobilization emerges on the basis of a collective gender identity, it cannot account for or address the different and complicated ways in which women make their gender identity. Finally, when lesbianism is offered as the only sexual position available to women who wish to refuse male control over their bodies, how women negotiate their heterosexuality is left unexplored. A "symptomatic reading" of the text of Lynne's response to the inclusion of lesbianism as a topic for an introductory Women's Studies course reveals the traces of particularity inherent in the psychic work of making identity in relation to the prohibitions and imperatives of the impossibility of the "feminine" position. It comes as no surprise that such work, which for the most part is performed at the level of the unconscious, becomes visible precisely at a moment of profound vulnerability.

It is, however, when we consider the relationship between Lynne's response and the identificatory positions she has been offered that "symptomatic reading" becomes a valuable analytic tool for curriculum theory. Lynne's contradictory response to the lesbian, which denies the lesbian's claim to the category of women and to the category of feminists, can be read as a response to the contradictory positions that the lesbian occupies within the curriculum of Women's Studies. One position situates the lesbian as feminism's magical sign; a second position situates the lesbian within feminism's history of privileging the experiences and interests of white, middle-class, heterosexual women.

Figured as feminism's magical sign, the lesbian appears to offer women new identificatory positions that refuse ideal femininity. However, to return to Wittig's sly conclusion, we are reminded that this work to create new identificatory positions cannot be reduced to one category (lesbians) in relation to its own constitutive limit category (women). Let us read her statement as a grammatical whole: "Lesbians are not women, no more is any woman who is not in a relation of personal dependency with a man" (110–111). Wittig insists upon examining the material effects of conceptual categories as well as economic relations of power. The lesbian she offers can be seen as a kind of battle cry that wanders between risking and refusing what King refers to as the trap of seeing lesbianism as feminism's magical sign.[5] By asking us to consider identity as a relation to both conceptual categories and practices, Wittig poses the question of what it means to make and claim positions as identity. This, it seems to me, could be a question of ongoing interest for feminist education. Ironically, given Wittig's antipathy to psychoanalytic theories, her assertion that lesbians are not women can be read against Jacques Lacan's (1998) famous assertion, *La femme n'existe pas*. Just as "woman" exists as an ideal category to which women must make a relation, "lesbian" can also be recognized as a category of identity that is "ideal" to the political demands of feminism, at least as Wittig understands them at the time of writing. Lynne's story requires us to pay close attention to the complicated ways in which individuals make and remake their identities in relation to the fictions of ideal categories of identity, including those offered by feminist discourses.

Lynne's story also demonstrates that the two categories of the tolerant and the tolerated imagined within an ideology of representational visibility are insufficient to make sense of how representation works at the level of identificatory processes. Lynne refuses lesbian difference, but her staging of this refusal is not organized by a concern for or even an interest in feminism's history of exclusions. Rather, her refusal is staged as a more personal and intimate dynamic of warding off a perceived threat to her identity.[6] What she resists when she resists lesbian difference is the failure of her identity as a woman to secure an image of itself as natural, cohesive, and originating in the self. This, as Wittig implies, is the risk and possibility of feminism, but Lynne has had little opportunity or even need to explore such an idea.

A symptomatic reading of students' engagement with feminist knowledge within Women's Studies helps us to examine what is at stake in the curricular selections and sequencing and in the pedagogical imperatives that operate there. Such a reading invites interpretations that reveal the anxieties and contradictions inherent in the pedagogical positions assumed by the course and that allow us to exceed these positions. In this case, a symptomatic reading asks to consider the limits of the sociological push to connect representation, with its emphasis on voice, experience, and visibility with bodies. Using the strategies of symptomatic reading we begin to see the need to understand the role of fantasy in the work that individuals do to render their identities as coherent and as relevant to learning. This is so whether we are students or teachers.

These strategies, as I have developed them here, may, however, be untranslatable to the day-to-day of classroom life. There are several reasons for this. One reason concerns the inevitable delay between the emergence of a set of curricular and pedagogical imperatives and our capacity to perceive the "conflicts inhering in a collective situation" (Gallop 1992, 7). A second reason concerns the qualities of research into classroom dynamics. The content of the research story I discuss in this chapter was not available to the instructors of the course. This may be so because, as Constance Penley (1989) notes, "the student can always sense the hidden demands of the teacher or parent. The student...is almost clairvoyant when it comes to understanding the desire of the Other and how best narcissistically to mirror what the Other desires." (169)

The problem is that it is difficult to learn the features of our hidden demands from our students if, for instance, we believe we know in advance the meaning of their silences or the purpose of their strategies of refusing the topics we have organized for discussion. Unfortunately, such beliefs privilege a theory of knowledge over a theory of learning. The theory of learning

I am advocating here requires that we become curious about *symptoms* of engagement in our work with students. As we do so, we may be able to conceive of the work of pedagogy as the work of creating conditions of learning where everyone is invited to study the structure of her response to the representations we offer. Such an invitation might begin with the study of the phantasmatic ideals embedded within these representations. In this exploration, an essay such as Wittig's "The Straight Mind" might be examined, not because it *represents* lesbians or problematizes normalization of heterosexuality. Such an essay might be engaged for the interesting ways it allows us to think about representations of gender and sexual identities as sites of identification where our phantasmatic ideals might be called into question, assessed, and perhaps even reconfigured.

Notes

1. The status of the lesbian may be equally, though differently, problematic in the emerging field of Gay and Lesbian Studies. As Judith Butler (1994) (see also Martin 1994 and Walters 1996) has pointed out, the emerging field of Lesbian and Gay Studies may owe political and theoretical allegiance to feminist theory, but there has been a tendency to define this field as offering theories of sexuality in contradistinction to feminist studies, which offers theories of gender. Butler worries about how the definitional demands of institutionality work against the productivity of holding questions and issues of gender and sexuality in tension with each other. Her concern, in my view, is a valid one, and perhaps my questions about conflicts within Women's Studies that stick to the figure of the lesbian can be viewed as a different form of this new concern. Wittig was one of several theorists, including Adrienne Rich, to place the social construction of sexuality as a problem of and for gender identity on the feminist agenda. Both appear, as do many other feminist theorists, between the pages of *The Lesbian and Gay Studies Reader* (1993).

2. It should be pointed out that Wittig, who, in this same essay, refuses psychoanalytic theory in general and the category of the unconscious in particular, may hold the view that her work (fictional and theoretical) is to elaborate aspects of women's social imaginary that already exist and to make these representations more widely available as a political project. But the "use" of representation can neither be guaranteed in advance nor permanently fixed to the goals of its historical moment of production (Simon 1992).

3. In other words, while this strategy of interpretation uses psychoanalytic categories, it is not the same as the psychoanalytic dialogue. Where the analyst offers interpretations that the analysand (the person in analysis) uses to enlarge, elaborate, and evaluate her own history, my interpretations are useful to readers interested in their practices of theorizing curriculum and pedagogy.

4. In one of her journal entries, Lynne describes her desire to recognize herself in images of women that exceed normative ideals of femininity. She considers this work to be necessary to the work of healing in the aftermath of her divorce, an event that has separated her physically and emotionally from her children, but she worries that she will "self-destruct" in the process. When Women's Studies relies upon knowledge to transform learners, it may not sufficiently take into account the difficult knowledge (see Britzman 1998) women already hold about their condition as female in a sexist society.

5. King's designation of lesbianism as feminism's magical sign is reminiscent of Donald Winnicott's understanding of "magical thinking" (see Phillips 1988). For this psychoanalyst, the baby believes that she produces the mother (or a feed) merely by wishing it, thus assuring herself of her omnipotence at a time when knowledge of her profound dependency would be overwhelming.

6. This does not mean, of course, that Lynne's response is unimplicated in the repetition of heterosexual women's anxieties about lesbianism. The problem concerns the pedagogical assumption that knowledge about this history is all students need in order to disentangle themselves.

Chapter Three

Qualifying Resistance: Some Comments on Methodological Dilemmas

"Resistance," in critical educational studies, is a curious concept. It can consider emancipatory hopes, where critical knowledge can be made from the refusal of official discourse. It can also consider the limits of these hopes, where pedagogical attempts to persuade large groups of people to become active participants in struggles against oppression fail. Resistance moves both ways, and, given its polymorphous nature, the study of resistance cannot escape this structural ambivalence. Whether the study of resistance points the researcher in the direction of pedagogical cure or in the direction of pedagogical critique, there is a common interest in locating resistance on the side of human agency. In whatever direction the act of interpreting research stories as stories of resistance tries to settle, there is still the dilemma of how to think about the gap between the research participant's interpretive framing of experience and the researcher's interpretive retelling of a story about experience. This gap is made from the play of other forms of ambivalence that take shape within human agency and between speaking subjects. This chapter explores the potential psychoanalytic theory offers, not to close that gap between the narration of experience and its interpretation but to examine it more closely.

Two questions organize my exploration of the meaning of resistance for research. First, what do we learn when we conceptualize resistance as a problem of and for interpretation? A second question takes up the problem of how we understand what representation means in research (Britzman 1995b; Lather 1991). How do our understandings change when we bring psychoanalytic notions of resistance to bear upon the telling and retelling of research stories? These questions began in my study of women's engagement with academic feminist knowledge (Pitt 1995). In this research, I investigated how student stories of engagement help us to examine the pedagogical positions offered by an introductory Women's Studies course. My study draws upon the complexities of classroom dynamics that are richly documented in the literature on feminist pedagogy (Briskin & Coulter 1992; Bunch & Pollack 1983; Culley & Portuges 1985; Luke & Gore 1992; Maher & Thompson Tetreault 1994).

Within this literature, the polymorphous nature of resistance figures prominently. In one direction, Women's Studies identifies itself with the political opposition of the women's movement. In another direction, debates that address the history of exclusions within the women's movement are played out in issues of curriculum and institutional hiring practices. And, in yet a third direction, the positive and negative responses of students are explored in relation to the range of demands associated with the first two directions. While resistance points in many directions, it is still possible, within this literature, to distinguish between "good" and "bad" stories of resistance.

The methodological questions that I explore in this chapter concern my dilemmas about interpreting students' reflections on how learning feminism organized and disorganized their understandings of what it means to be a woman in a sexist society. I began my original research with a question of how a psychoanalytic conceptualization of resistance (Felman 1987) might enrich our understandings of what was at stake in students' refusals of feminist knowledge. This was prompted by an interest in discovering the meaning of resistance for the students. I was, however, unprepared for the ways in which psychoanalytic approaches to reading resistance would also transform my own understanding of how resistance works in the telling and retelling of narratives about learning and not learning, in this case, feminism. When learning is conceptualized as a psychical process, the boundaries between "good" and "bad" stories of resistance blur, and a new question emerges: What is the meaning of resistance for learning?

What I had not anticipated were the implications of a psychoanalytic notion of resistance that has little to do with the attributes of an individual's actions or behaviors. Rather, resistance in a psychoanalytic sense refers to processes of managing psychic conflict. From this perspective, resistance is a method. While the psychoanalytic story that resistance tells may begin with a resounding "no" in the face of new and difficult knowledge, this "no" conceals a much more ambivalent story of implication in the very knowledge that one is at pains to refuse. The problem is not that psychoanalytic theories complicate the "no." These complications were, after all, what drew my attention to the potential of psychoanalysis for my research. The problem is that psychoanalytic theories complicate all of our stories of engagement with knowledge by insisting upon the role of unconscious processes in the making of such stories. These complications reside within knowledge itself, and they circulate in the stories told to us, in our retellings of them as research stories, and in our readings of such retellings. They ask us to consider not only what we can know as we work with these four dynamics of meaning-making but also how our will and desire not to know can be exchanged, interpreted, and worked through.

Psychoanalytic understandings of story resonate with poststructuralist notions of the relationship between experience and its narration. Joan Scott (1992) describes this relationship and its implications for historiography when she argues that:

> (...) we need to attend to the historical processes that, through discourse, position subjects and produce their experiences. It is not individuals who have experience, but subjects who are constituted through experience. Experience in this definition then becomes not the origin of our explanation, not the authoritative (because seen or felt) evidence that grounds what is known, but rather that which we seek to explain, that about which knowledge is produced. (25–26)

Where poststructuralist theories invert the humanistic notion that we name our experience as we narrate it, psychoanalytic theories further unseat the authority of the humanist subject by insisting upon the notion of the unconscious. There is, both within the subject and its narrative desires, something that resists itself, something that escapes the consolations of rationality and intentionality. Thus, the psychoanalytic subject emerges as simultaneously constituted by social processes of signification and as an effect of residual and unresolved psychic conflicts. In addition to asking how we can represent the experience of others in our research—a question provoked by poststructuralist concerns, we must also ask how we can understand the experience of representing versions of self, both in the stories we tell to others and in those we retell as research stories.

This chapter begins with a brief history of the concept of resistance in educational research read through the lens of psychoanalytic theories that call into question our capacity to distinguish psychical response from social context. Wherever educational study relies upon the category of resistance to identify behaviours, attitudes, and actions, it may be important to examine how psychoanalytic notions consider the qualities and dynamics of ambivalence within resistance. What does it mean to think of resistance as method? With this question I bring a psychoanalytically inflected notion of resistance to bear on a reading of a research story as a means to pressure the theoretical claims at stake. Of the five case studies constituting my original research, the story I focus on here best represents my struggles to come to terms with my own resistance to the notion of resistance offered by psychoanalytic theory. In the conclusion, I reconsider the value of this research story for my exploration of academic feminist education and raise some questions about what a psychoanalytically inflected understanding of resistance means for critical educational research.

Some Comments on the Construct of Resistance in Education Theory

Early on, Henry Giroux (1983) argued for a critical science of education interested in resistance as a form of behavior that opposes the demands and expectations of institutions. Giroux offered three compelling reasons. First, seeing oppositional behaviors as resistance interrupts practices of interpretation that define such behavior as deviant or as the effects of learned helplessness. Second, the identification of resistance allows educational theorists to elaborate a more fluid understanding of the relation between human agency and social constraint. And, third, as a heuristic device, theories of resistance can function as an antidote to the pessimism of reproduction theories that were then dominant in educational theory. Because reproduction theories valorize the structural determination of inequality in education, a focus on resistance as opposed to compliance can be interpreted as expressing hope for radical social change.

However, even as Giroux (1983) welcomed the value of resistance for developing a more nuanced critical theory of education, he insisted that the interpretation of resistance poses new methodological problems for research. Giroux warned against over-zealous identifications of oppositional behavior with radical intentionality and offered suggestions for heightening the analytical precision of the use of resistance as a theoretical construct. Such precision requires:

> (...) a theoretical starting point that links the display of behaviour to the interest it embodies, going beyond the immediacy of behaviour to the interest that underlies its often hidden logic, a logic that must be interpreted through the historical and cultural mediations that shape it. (291)

Interpretations of resistance must distinguish among those acts of resistance that embody nascent radical potential, those that stand in opposition to hegemonic values but manage also to foreclose opportunities for consciousness-raising and critical action, and, finally, those that reveal a struggle against one dimension of structural inequality but enact an unexamined reliance upon one or more other dimensions (for an ethnography of these dynamics, see Weis 1990).

The lads in Paul Willis' (1977) classic ethnography offer a familiar example of the complexities involved in exploring issues of resistance. These young men refused to valorize literacy over manual labor. The problem is that the autonomy that produces the lads' refusal in effect returns them to a dependency on the existing social order and their position within it. This nonautonomous autonomy also, as Angela McRobbie (1991) and others have pointed out, relies upon the unthought of unequal social relations of gender. The lads resist their own implication in relations of everyday power that make the lives of the girls and women they encounter more difficult. But there is also something more that the lads resist. Near the end of the study Willis still attempts to engage them in what he believes to be emancipatory thought. The lads reject these attempts, and they tell Willis as much, thus resisting Willis' own dreams for the emancipatory potential of research.

Still, to return to Giroux's point, while oppositional behavior can signify an individual's potential for autonomous action, the term "resistance" should be able to say something about an individual's commitments. The practical suggestions Giroux offers encourage the researcher to contextualize her interpretive claims in history and culture and in the microsocial relations of each individual. While narratives of resistance continue to be significant for the study of the complex ways in which individuals make sense of experience (see, for instance, Munro 1996; Weiler 1992), it is important to consider the full measure of Scott's claims cited earlier, that all analyses of experience must be situated within a larger discursive arena. If narratives of resistance do not transcend but rather implicate their narrator within discursive frames of intelligibility, then Giroux's guidelines may not fully solve the methodological dilemmas inherent in interpreting resistance in research stories. There is still the danger of finding resistance in all the wrong places and the problem of considering the issues opened when the study of resistance attributes meanings to actions that do correspond and do not correspond to the meanings actors attribute to them. While qualitative studies admit that interpretation is not limited to the sense actors make of their experience, there is still something quite troubling about positing the researcher's interpretations as having the capacity to tell the truth about the meaning of an action of another. Psychoanalytic views, though, consider the fault lines of the researcher's inadvertent attribution of either positive or negative agency onto the subject as a problem of and for desire. The limits of Giroux's interpretive model to think through this problem become more evident when we consider the ways in which critical, feminist, and antiracist pedagogies provoke resistance on the part of the very learners they seek to address. How do we understand the dynamics of refusing knowledge?

These pedagogies begin with the assumption that individual consciousness proceeds from the possession of the truth grounded in knowledge of their social condition. In recent research stories of learners' engagement with counter-hegemonic pedagogies, researchers have become quite concerned with developing strategies for interpreting the learner's refusals to take up the knowledge on offer. What happens, for example, when some learners do not believe that inequality matters? What happens when people suffer from forces that are beyond their control? These pedagogies, and the subject positions they articulate, introduce learners to formalized bodies of knowledge that privilege the perspectives and experiences of oppressed and socially marginalized identities on the assumption that such knowledge will provide more satisfying and truthful ways for learners to respond to the question, "Who am I?"

But when learners refuse to recognize themselves within the subject positions on offer, critical educators are confronted with the need to theorize forms of resistance that are, at least at first glance, qualitatively different from those forms identified in Giroux's earlier review of critical educational literature. In our present time, there seem to be two orientations to this dilemma. In the research on teacher education, for example, researchers locate the barrier of resistance somewhere between the agency of the individual and dominant ideology (Cochran-Smith 1993; Ladson-Billings 1996; Sleeter 1993; Zeichner & Liston 1991). This orientation is also evident in much recent writing about feminist classrooms that focuses on struggles over the meanings of race, class, and sex for the analysis and experience of gender oppression (Bannerji, Carty, Dehli, Heald & McKenna 1991; Martindale 1992).

A second group of theorists, mainly concerned with a broader view of educational studies, locate the barrier of resistance somewhere between the individual and her capacity to act upon transformative knowledge. In a move that owes a great deal to poststructuralist theories of subject formation, this second group of educational researchers (Bogdan 1994; Britzman 1992; Ellsworth 1989; Lewis 1990; Lather 1991; Luke & Gore 1992; McCarthy 1990; Simon 1992) theorize both directions of student resistance in relation to counter-hegemonic knowledge by beginning with the assumption that resistance against emancipatory knowledge cannot be reduced to the residual and passive effects of "false consciousness." In very different ways this second orientation suggests that resistance in the classroom is symptomatic of discontinuities in teaching and learning that are not easily reconciled with a theory of learning that assumes the Freirean continuity between the experience of oppression and the experience of learning about oppression (for a discussion of this dilemma, see Weiler 1991).

Two themes characterize this complex body of work. One theme asks us to consider the ways in which new knowledge does disrupt learners' prior self-understandings, but instead of producing feelings of empowerment, these disruptions are experienced as producing new and often debilitating forms of helplessness and isolation. A second theme concerns the ways in which our very efforts to create learning conditions designed to empower marginalized populations can both reproduce the effects of social inequality and conceal a pedagogical will to dominate. What these themes and the location of resistance within them suggest is that a theory of resistance must be able to engage, not only the ways in which acts of resistance are attached to the social, but also the ways in which individuals—as teachers, learners, and researchers—are attached to resistance.

These theorists reformulate Giroux's insistence that we examine the historical conditions and material social investments that underlie oppositional actions. Rather than asking what potential acts of individual resistance hold for collective political intervention, these theorists ask what resistance to knowledge does for individuals who must negotiate social conditions that are not of their own making. A new layer of interpretation is introduced when the context of the classroom is viewed as implicated in the very social relations it hopes to observe, analyze, and disrupt. Here, resistance represents a mode of interpretative negotiation of the social as it is lived in classrooms. Still, the methodological dilemma of how to see an action as resistance persists for those of us concerned with the gap between the interpretive framing of experience and its interpretive staging as a research story.

This is particularly evident in Lather's (1991) study of women's engagement in an introductory Women's Studies course, which is presented as an exploration of the implications of "postmodern theories" for qualitative research methodologies. Her observation that researchers tell research stories in theoretical forms that determine how data are selected, organized, and interpreted calls into question the privileging of theoretical precision recommended by Giroux but may not resolve the problem of what resistance means in research stories. Lather's examination of student's resistances to emancipatory pedagogies resides in the question of "what these resistances have to teach us about our own impositional tendencies" (76). Thus, Lather suggests that resistance is a relation and not an attribute of individual intentionality. But there is another problem that Lather does not consider. What if the students' resistance exceeds the teachers' efforts or speaks from a place of prior history rather than present relation?

These recent approaches to theorizing resistance hold onto the tensions among classroom dynamics, curricular investments, and the investments of learners and teachers. What they share is a curiosity about the ways in which resistance on the part of learners interrupts critical theoretical assumptions about the relations between the realm of the social and the reproductive/productive interventions of educational practices. They both ask, in other words, how educational research can account for resistance and how individual acts of resistance can be directed towards larger goals of collective struggles against inequality. They insist that resistance is evidence of active negotiation with social demands, the interpretation of which both requires and revises theory. But what if, as Lather's study suggests, the story of desire that resistance tells is incommensurable with the story of desire that educational researchers tell about resistance? Moreover, what if the methodological dilemma I have described in terms of the meaning of resistance actually presents us with a larger dilemma of what it means to ground our research claims in the stories others tell about their experiences?

Psychoanalysis and the Problem of Interpretation

Psychoanalytic theory offers us a way into the problem of interpretation that centers the implications of desire for interpretive practices. The story of desire that resistance tells in psychoanalysis is also contexualized by history, but this history situates the struggle to gain self-knowledge in that intimate and profoundly personal space of the individual psyche. Taking a cue from recent studies that explore the vicissitudes of learning when learning is conceptualized as a psychic event (Britzman 1998; Britzman & Pitt 1996; Felman 1987; Finke 1993; Gallop 1995b; Robertson 1997; Todd 1996), this chapter asks what it might mean to consider the telling and retelling of research stories as narratives of psychic events. Resistance, in this narrative version, does not occupy the same place as it does for the two approaches to understanding resistance outlined above. Where these approaches locate resistance when the subject meets the otherness of ideology or its critique, a psychoanalytic story locates resistance where the subject meets the otherness of her own unconscious knowledge.

Shoshana Felman (1987) gives us some idea of what is entailed in thinking about research stories as psychic events involving unconscious as well as conscious meanings. She opens her discussion of the implications of psychoanalysis for education with the observation that, for Jacques Lacan, "the unconscious...is grounded not so much in an ontological as in an ethical experience" (69). She quotes from Lacan's *Seminaire XI*:

> The status of the unconscious, which, as I have suggested, is so fragile on the ontic plane, is ethical: in his thirst for truth, Freud says, *Whatever may happen, it is imperative to go there.* (69, emphasis in the original)

Freud, as we well know, spent his life going there, and he learned, among other things, that the unconscious is a destination that one never quite reaches. One's arrival is always deferred and delayed but not only because the unconscious is complicated and difficult to grasp with our meagre tools. One never arrives because the unconscious is dynamic, forever creating itself anew from the bits and pieces of everyday life that remind us of wishes that are taboo and experiences that are too painful to confront head on. It is the dynamic quality of the unconscious that makes running after it an experience that is ethical rather than ontological. The truth it tells is never quite the truth about ourselves but a stranger and perhaps intolerable form of truth: the truth that we can't be the masters of our self-knowledge.

Still, the psychoanalytic encounter begins with Freud's insistence, "*Whatever may happen, it is imperative to go there.*" It begins there because, as Freud suggests, people suffer from their reminiscences. If all goes well, one's immediate suffering is relieved, and one learns something about how to replicate the conditions of analysis without the benefit of the analyst. This, too, is part of the ethicality of psychoanalytic practice (Horney 1942). We might say that psychoanalytic learning consists of two parts. One part deals with the curious ways in which ideas and affect organize and reorganize each other and attach themselves to new experiences. This part is particular to the life history and disposition of the individual. The other part deals with methodological questions: How to go there? What does it mean to think about representing the stories of others as bound up with the ethical demands of running after something as elusive as the split subject of psychoanalysis? In which direction shall one run?

In order to "go there" one must pass through resistance, and, for this reason, the study of resistance is central to psychoanalytic method. Early in his career Freud believed that his patients' resistances to his interpretations of their dreams and symptoms emanated from the barriers constructed by the unconscious to protect what lay hidden there—repressed from consciousness. Later, as with so many of his theoretical insights, he changed his mind about the relationship between repression and resistance. Where he had assumed that repressed knowledge protects itself from discovery by erecting a barrier of resistance, his work with patients forced him to revise this view and to argue instead that the patient's resistance to unconscious knowledge was enacted by the ego as a defense against such knowledge. The unconscious, he writes, "has no other endeavour than to break through the pressure weighing down on it and force its way either to consciousness or to a discharge through some real action" (1920, 19). It is this notion of resistance as a mechanism of defense against unconscious knowledge and the entanglements of implication that might offer educational research a different lens for reading resistance in research stories.

Laplanche and Pontalis (1973) describe the work of resistance in analysis: "the defensive mechanisms directed against former danger recur in the treatment as resistance against recovery. It follows from this that *the ego treats recovery itself as a new danger*" (396, emphasis added). What kind of danger might psychoanalytic treatment pose to the analysand? Is it possible that a similar danger haunts the telling of stories, not only in the context of research but in the context of everyday life as well? Let us take a closer look at how psychoanalysis approaches psychoanalytic learning and story-telling.

The analyst is interested in a particular kind of knowledge, that is, unconscious knowledge or, in Lacan's words, "knowledge that cannot tolerate one's knowing that one knows" (cited in Felman 1987, 77). The analyst believes that, even though the analysand cannot speak about her unconscious knowledge, the unconscious nevertheless speaks. Thus, the analyst assumes that the stories people tell always say more than they mean and never mean exactly what they say. In this way, then, a psychoanalytic story is understood as exceeding a representation of events; such a story is understood to be *an event in its own right.* For Roy Schafer (1983, 1992), narration belongs to the realm of the performance of identity:

> We are forever telling stories about ourselves. In telling these stories to others we may...be said to perform straightforward narrative actions. In saying that we also tell them to ourselves, however, we are enclosing one story within another....On this view, the self is a telling. (1983, 218–19)

The construction of a self-narrative in analysis engages unconscious meanings and wishes, and this engagement transforms the self that narrates. Self-transformation is the creative and dialogic work of analysis. It is creative because it is particular to the inter- and intrapersonal dynamics of the participants. It part, it is dialogic because it requires the active presence of two selves in dialogue. It is, however, also dialogic in that psychoanalytic theory and psychoanalytic practice are set in tension with each other. The analyst proceeds on the basis of her generalized theoretical knowledge at the same time as it is the analysand's self-knowledge, conscious and unconscious, that provides the material for interpretation. The gap between the analysand's interpretive framing of her experience and the analyst's interpretive retelling of the analysand's story about her experience constitutes the pedagogical space of psychoanalysis.

If we rewrite the last sentence, with some substitutions, we might bring into sharper focus its relevance for research. The gap between the participant's interpretive framing of her experience and the researcher's interpretive retelling of the participant's story about her experience constitutes the pedagogical space of research. Two moments and, hence, two potential spaces are implied in research. One location is the space between the researcher and the participant. Here the researcher's interpretive work occurs in the immediacy of the encounter and returns to the participant for further consideration. A second location lies in the space between the researcher's interpretive retelling and a community that shares an interest in the dilemmas under consideration. The movement between these two spaces constitutes the time of research. In neither context can the goal be one of recovering unconscious and repressed material. This work, and the particular risk it involves, must remain the purview of the psychoanalytic dialogue. How this space is conceptualized might have implications for a psychoanalytically informed understanding of what it means to learn and not learn. It might also have implications for what it means to interpret the narratives of others. In the next section, I discuss Schafer's formulations of the psychoanalytic life history and its implications for research.

Psychoanalytic Life History: The Means and the Ends of "Cure"

Schafer (1983) describes Freudian analysis as a life-historical discipline. The life history that is produced in analysis shares many features with poststructuralist renderings of life history within social science research. Both disciplines begin with the assumption that telling stories about our life experiences is imbricated in the work of identity formation, and both are interested in issues concerning deception, resistance, and contradictions. Still, these two kinds of stories rely on very different ways of understanding what it means to take these issues into account.

George Rosenwald and Richard Ochberg (1992) describe the implications of the poststructuralist turn in the social sciences:

> The dismantling of the realist position has shattered the image of life stories as the mirror of life events. When Allport, Shaw, or Lewis reported life histories—how one episode of a life leads coherently into another—that coherence was assumed to dwell within the events themselves.... We now believe that at least in the worlds of psychological and social consciousness, coherence is imposed by the work of the story makers.... The logic with which one event leads into another is not simply "out there," waiting to be recognized by any disinterested observer. Instead, coherence derives from the tacit assumptions of plausibility that shape the way each story weaves the fragmentary episodes of experience into a history. (3)

Like the social science life history, the analytic version is interested in the "coherence" of the plot and the structural organization of the past from the vantage of the present. However, for the social scientist one of the interpretive goals of the researcher is to reveal the cultural and ideological investments that produce the narrative structure and its narrator as coherent. Like the analyst, the social scientist listens for what must be forgotten, contradicted, and refused in order for the illusion of narrative coherence to be maintained. For the analyst, however, these forgettings, contradictions, and refusals implicate the unconscious of the individual psyche rather than the hegemonic traces of dominant ideology in the unacknowledged aspects of the past that are covered over by claims of coherence. This is an important distinction.

Both the social scientist and the analyst are concerned with what cannot be acknowledged within the human need to produce a coherent story of one's life. However, the analyst hears a claim about identity that seems quite different from the one the social scientist hears. The identity claims heard by the social scientist cast the story of becoming in terms of a progression from the past to the present, where the meanings of past events and understandings are reinterpreted and reintegrated into more current understandings. On this view, memory is constantly revisited, revised, and, in the process, the sum of who one imagines oneself to be is reformulated from the vantage of the present. In contrast, the identity claims heard by the analyst are marked by the persistence of a belief on the part of the analysand in *radical discontinuity* between one's past and one's present. Here, memory does not function as a device, however unreliable, for ordering one's self-narrative as a story of developmental and experiential progression. Rather, memory is the means by which belief in a developed and experienced sense of self is secured. And deception, for the analyst, has less to do with the faultiness of memory as record keeper than it has to do with self-deceiving, unconscious processes of repression. The fault lines of memory, on this view, are organized by the material of unconscious conflicts—the theoretical knowledge of psychoanalysis—that have never been admissible to conscious memory.

Schafer's unapologetic description of the intertextuality between life experience and psychoanalytic interpretation is precisely what critics of psychoanalytic method argue is the trap of psychoanalysis. Simply put, the critics charge psychoanalysis is capable of seeing only what it is looking for. This, as we have seen, is also the circularity of resistance theory in critical studies of education. We might say that a persistent problem for both psychoanalysis and education concerns not just the interminable exchange between learning from theory and learning from practice but the question of how work with subjectivity can be outside the workings of subjectivity. Still, when it comes to questions of resistance, the psychoanalyst and the researcher proceed very differently. Where the researcher asks what the implications of resistance are for education, the psychoanalyst asks how both participants in the psychoanalytic dialogue are implicated in the dynamics of resistance that flow back and forth between the unconscious of one subject and the unconscious of another.

As we listen to stories told to us in the context of research, we might remember that self-narration is a particular kind of work by means of which something is achieved for our participants that lies in radical excess of what they intend by their narratives. Self-narration exceeds as well what motivates them to produce a narrative for research (see Scheurich 1995). In turn, as we interpret their stories, we find that we, too, are working in the only way possible for us in that curious time where theory, interpretation, and psychic/social dynamics of life history inform each other and also turn back on each other. These relations, where blindness and insight act upon and through each other, are not merely the work identity does; these relations constitute the identities at work.

Research Stories and the Question of Implication

Psychoanalytic theory breaks with the tradition of equating being with presence—however complicated by degrees and forms of social difference—by asserting an identity formed in relation to others and self-otherness. Rather than asking what people learn from our pedagogical efforts, psychoanalytic understandings of identity formation suggest that we attend to questions of how people learn. The interesting question is not *what* the researcher learns from narrative accounts but *how* we learn from these accounts. We begin to see the consequences of organizing classrooms and research methods within frames that privilege a view that posits the prior existence of identities of either researchers or research participants. Whether such frames locate resistance on the side of agency or as an effect of false consciousness, they continue to perceive resistance as the consequence of not being addressed.

If, however, we begin with notions of identity as relation and resistance as the dynamics of the ego's refusal of the address of its own unconscious knowledge, we must ask very different questions of research stories and their interpretations. What happens if the stories we tell about ourselves (and to ourselves) are understood as attempts to fulfill the impossible desire to see ourselves? What if these stories fail to represent us to the other and represent instead our failure to represent ourselves to the other and for the other? And how do these questions implicate the researcher as the listener and reteller of the stories of others? In order to take up these questions, I turn to excerpts from a story told to me in the context of my study (Pitt 1995) of how women engage feminist knowledge in an introductory Women's Studies course. My study was limited to the students' perceptions of their own engagement and breakdowns in the course. I was not the teacher.

The research participants who volunteered were enrolled in a second-year-level course offered by the college for part-time studies at a large urban university. The college attracts both full- and part-time students, which means that the age range represented is greater than that of traditional full-time students. The course provides one means to satisfy pre-requisite requirements for upper-level Women's Studies courses and counts towards a Women's Studies major. Issues, such as violence, work, and sexuality, are approached from a range of theoretical perspectives, and a wide variety of fictional and nonfictional accounts of women's experiences is offered.

Five women volunteered to participate in my study, which drew data from three sources. Participants kept a journal in which they recorded their impressions of the course readings and films, their observations about classroom dynamics, and their own participation in class discussions, and their ideas about how the course was affecting their perspectives on what it means to be a woman and a feminist. There was no journal requirement for the course, and the journal writing that participants produced for me was neither read nor evaluated by the course instructors. A second source of data was copies of the written assignments for the course. Open-ended interviews comprised the third source of data. I interviewed each participant twice individually, and three of the participants also met with me once as a group.

The Interminability of Telling the Self

Tanis, a white, heterosexual woman in her mid-to-late thirties, was one of the women who participated in my study. She is the sole support of a teenage daughter and the first member of her working-poor family to go to university. In the following journal entry, she describes some of what participation in an introductory Women's Studies course means to her:

> Taking Women's Studies courses is a revelation of my true self. It helps me understand why I feel the things I do, explains those feelings and as a result, I feel whole, special, at peace with myself.
>
> There is a gentleness to courses of this nature. Being taught by women who naturally teach by talking, calmly, peacefully, is so exciting. It makes me want to know more and more. Like a child listening to an adventure story. For discovering yourself is really an adventure.

The adventure of self-discovery that Tanis describes is organized by her engagement with the epistemological framework of academic feminism. This epistemological framework considers feminism, in all of its theoretical and perspectival diversity, as a way of knowing that centers women's experiences and perspectives and as a knowledge base that formalizes these experiences and perspectives within and against more traditional disciplines and textual genres. It also frames feminist knowledge as a politics of collective and individual action of resistance against oppression. This is the resistance of resistance theory. What I came to consider in the course of my return to Tanis' journal entry is that this epistemological framework also sets the terms by which teachers and students recognize themselves as participants.

As I suggest earlier in this chapter, I was curious about how stories of engagement might help us to investigate the pedagogical positions offered by introductory Women's Studies courses. I began the research with an interest in how students' responses might illuminate how these pedagogical positions were shaped by tensions within Women's Studies (and academic feminisms more generally) between the desire to unite women and the need to acknowledge differences among women. Rather than understanding these stories as bothering the aims of feminist education, I was interested in how they bother and are bothered by the subject positions that Women's Studies offers as sites of student/teacher recognition. Thus, I believed that I would learn more about the subject positions offered within Women's Studies from students who refused to occupy them.

This is the second force of resistance that I discussed in the introduction, and it shaped my belief that resistance could be considered as a response to feelings of being misrecognized or unaddressed. Consequently, I initially believed that Tanis' journal writings and interviews held little relevance for my study for, in this entry, she focused on her feelings of being spoken to. As long as my attention was focused on the meanings imposed on students by the curriculum, I could not attend to the ways in which students' impositions of their own meanings shape their learning from the curriculum. However, by bringing psychoanalytic conceptualizations of learning and resistance to bear on my reading of Tanis' story, I was able to learn something about my own investments in the "good story" of feminist pedagogy and something as well about the value of reading research stories more analytically.

Let us return to Tanis as she continues to elaborate the pleasures of her adventure of self-discovery, thereby constituting herself as a "good student" of academic feminism, that is, one who has little difficulty in recognizing herself as a woman within the terms of the course:

> (...) I say that Women's Studies truly allows women to study themselves, to study the meaning of being a woman. Women have studied what men study about men. It

> is distant, impersonal, most of which only the famous or elite could relate to. For the others it is just mindless idolatry. Men accept their image much the same way most women accept their own image of men and themselves.
>
> But through the study of that image, we begin to understand what is really happening, what the consequences are of accepting the image that has been prepared for us, and to decide what we are going to do about it now that the cold, hard facts have been slapped in our faces. For this reason I would say that men have always studied other men, have been so overwhelmed with the presence of other men in society and history that they did not even think to question, much the same way women have felt.
>
> I believe that if men were to study men in the same way a Women's Studies course is directed, they would have to come to terms with the fact that they are the oppressors of women, revealing their insecurities, and ignorance, and having to come to terms with it.

Tanis does not believe that men will relinquish their social power without a struggle, nor does she believe that they will easily alter their personal modes of interaction with women. But she does believe that she has nothing to lose and everything to gain by participating, in whatever way she can, in the struggle for women's equality. At the same time, Tanis may be "ready" to investigate some deeper questions about what it means to be a woman and a feminist.

If the central question of this course is, "Can I recognize myself as a woman within the terms of this course?," the question that might be more useful to Tanis would be, "What are the implications of recognizing myself as a woman within the framework of feminist epistemology?" By taking a closer look at the position Tanis produces for herself in her narratives—the self she tells, we can begin to discern some interesting contradictions that Tanis has had little opportunity to explore in the context of the course. Moreover, because my own investments in resistance as an oppositional force converged with those of the course in ways I had not understood at the time, my conversations with Tanis within the context of the research did little to exceed this constraint. Simply put, I could not hear the contradictions and, hence, did not invite elaboration. In another journal entry Tanis addresses her feelings of empowerment:

> Women's Studies gives me power—the power to relate on an equal level to anyone, regardless of class, race or sex. Of course it is particularly powerful when dealing with men. Why? Because I have knowledge of things that they don't have. This knowledge provides me with a unique understanding of reality and gives me a feeling of confidence that few people, and in particular, any man, could ever have.

> There are men that I associate with through business and personal relationships that are keenly interested in my new-found knowledge and I know that they appreciate learning something new through me. It's like a refreshingly intelligent, knowledgeable enlightenment for them. Because through me they are learning about themselves. How much of it sticks with them I can't say. But they never argue and they say that they really enjoy talking to me. Poor lost little creatures.

Tanis makes numerous references to men's insecurities, to their lack of self-awareness about the effects of their place within social relations of power, and to the need to educate men as well as to agitate for social change. Her sense of being in charge of herself is organized, in part, by her sense of being in charge of relationships with men. Tanis' desire to be in charge of her relationships with men began before she enrolled in university as a part-time student:

> My parents never had any expectations of us, except to be obedient perhaps. All of us four girls, to escape our meagre home life, married by the ages 18 and 19. We all became wives, mothers, and paid workers. Surprisingly, we managed to juggle all of that, but what really made us unhappy, angry, and sometimes severely depressed was that we couldn't have any kind of equality in our own homes; we couldn't even be who we really were but rather only what suited our husbands, and what suited our husbands, all of them, was that we be under their control.

The past tense in this journal excerpt is curious, and it signals one of the tensions just below the surface of this student's embrace of feminist knowledge. Tanis is the only one of her sisters to have left her husband. She has removed herself from conditions she has come to see as a repetition of her parents' abusive relationship in her own life. Tanis is proud of her achievements. She enjoys her university courses and her job; and the life she has been able to provide herself and her daughter is very different, both materially and emotionally, from her own life growing up. But the project of distancing herself from her life growing up may exact its own costs in the form of a certain kind of loneliness and alienation from her sisters, whom Tanis describes as unhappy but either unwilling or unable to change their lives. In the above journal excerpt, the use of the past tense and the pronoun "we" elides the differences among these women by bestowing upon them all the "consciousness" about their life conditions that Tanis claims for herself.

These women did share the difficult material conditions and emotional climate of their childhood, and their flight from those experiences seems to have had the unwelcome, but not uncommon, effect of repeating them. But the narrative coherence of this story relies upon the perspective of feminist discourse. Tanis creates the illusion that her perspective is one collectively shared by herself and her sisters, but she also explains her sisters' continuing troubles and unhappiness by insisting that they have not had access to feminist knowledge. Tanis believes that it is knowledge that has transformed her life. What this belief seems unable to admit is that feminist knowledge has provided her with a storyline to render her decisions and understandings coherent. On the assumption that knowledge produces transformation, Tanis takes her new knowledge into her relationships with both men and her sisters in the hopes that it will transform them as well.

One might still raise the question, what does this story have to do with resistance? At first glance, it seems that the story that Tanis tells is the "good" story of resistance where hegemonic meanings are refused and counter-hegemonic meanings are clearly articulated. Because Tanis has no difficulty in recognizing herself as a woman within the terms of the course, she is unlikely to draw the attention of a teacher or a researcher who worries that the desire to empower others conceals the teacher's will to power (Lather 1991). The will to power that is concealed within Tanis' feelings of empowerment is more intimate. It produces women as gentle; teaching and, hence, learning as calm (yet exciting); sisters as just like her, but in need of her knowledge; and men as "poor, lost little creatures," also in need of her knowledge.

These formulations may represent the familiar modes of emerging attachment to feminist discourse that prefer reversals over nuance and that take great pleasure in exploring familiar worlds with new lenses. On this view, the learner becomes more sophisticated over time as she moves through ways of knowing that privilege the subjective experience of the knower and those that privilege the authority of knowledge itself to more relational ways of knowing. Belenky, Clinchy, Goldberger & Tarule (1986) call this latter perspective "constructed knowledge" and describe it as "a position in which women view all knowledge as contextual, experience themselves as creators of knowledge, and value both subjective and objective strategies for knowing" (15).

When it comes to feminist knowledge, we must remember that such knowledge is by definition oppositional to and marginalized within dominant knowledge. We might ask ourselves if forging a relation to feminist knowledge is similar to making a relation to unconscious knowledge. If, as I suggested earlier in this chapter, psychoanalytic treatment poses new dangers to the analysand manifesting itself as resistance against recovery, we might also argue that feminist knowledge poses new dangers to the learner and that learning, like recovery, must pass through resistance. This supposition asks us to reconsider the contradictory moments within Tanis' expressions of empowerment as also expressions of uncertainty, doubt, and even loss that are covered over by the appeal to the authority of feminist knowledge.

Michael Eigen's (1986) discussion of the intimate relationship between knowing and experience can help us speculate on the meaning of resistance in Tanis' narrative. Our speculation, however, requires that we take a detour. We cannot ask what resistance, in the sense of a mechanism of defense against unconscious knowledge, means for Tanis. We can, however, ask what it means for feminist knowledge and how my encounter with Tanis was shaped by my own appeal to the authority of feminist knowledge.

Assuming the role of one who knows carries with it the danger of forgetting that others also work from their knowledge. Pushed to its extremes, knowing tips into omniscience, an inflated and delusional wish for limitless mental power. Eigen (1986) argues that "omniscience may be an empty pretension. But an onmiscience-inflated subject fills himself with a sense of infinite privilege and foists his personality on others instead of suffering limits in the struggle to know" (321). Eigen distinguishes between omniscience and its close relation, omnipotence (or limitless physical power), but also recognizes that they may operate in tandem as psychic defenses against helplessness.

Omniscience and omnipotence have their origins in a more archaic omnipotence that is a form of psychic defense against helplessness that we all, to some extent or another, rely upon in our daily lives. Both may also be relevant to forming deeper understandings of the limits of feminist knowledge as a personal and political weapon against women's oppression. Archaic omnipotence may be delusional, but at one point in our lives it was also necessary to our development. Omnipotence is necessary because the infant is utterly dependent upon the care of others for its very survival, and yet premature understanding of this dependence would result in stress too difficult to manage (see Winnicott 1971b). At the same time, learning to renounce omnipotence as delusional is integral to the formation of the infant as a social being. That is, the infant comes gradually to realize that her screams do not magically produce the longed-for feeding or comfort but rather act as a signal to the caregiver, who then responds. However, as Sheila Ernst (1989) points out, the fantasy of omnipotence may never be fully renounced and returns to haunt adult life in times of vulnerability.

When resistance masquerades as omnipotence, what is at stake is the refusal to admit the limits of one's real power. Elizabeth Grosz (1991) suggests that just such resistance may be necessary for and integral to feminist subjectivity. She argues that feminism itself "can be seen as a form of mass or collective psychosis, a political disavowal of women's social reality as oppressed" (39). Disavowal is a psychic mechanism of defense that turns on the incapacity to recognize a traumatic perception. In this contradictory space of psychic reality, one knows and does not know at exactly the same time. The political disavowal that Grosz refers to concerns the psychic reality that is the condition of feminism. The traumatic perception of women's oppression is feminism's grounds of necessity if political resistance is to be countenanced, but, at the same time, women must act as if they were not oppressed and hence in charge of their political destinies.

In the Women's Studies classroom, women are introduced to knowledge produced by and for women in the hopes that such knowledge will create new understandings of their own experiences as women and that these new understandings will lead to political mobilization. In this context, the learning that matters the most is learning to make a relation to feminist knowledge. We might say that, for the Women's Studies student, knowledge precedes action. Similarly, omniscience may precede omnipotence in relation to that curious formulation of feminist disavowal offered by Grosz (1991). In this formulation, as we have seen, helplessness and empowerment become entwined when knowledge about women's oppression is felt to be true at the same time as the remedies threaten to overwhelm the knower. The danger here is that knowledge can turn against the knower. As Eigen (1986) warns, "it is difficult to overestimate the role omniscience plays in deadening our capacity to experience" (320).

This is so because the degree of certainty and inviolability one brings to experience in terms of what and how one knows thwarts our capacity to know differently, to tolerate uncertainty, and to allow ourselves to be vulnerable to the possibility that our knowledge is partial and insufficient. Perhaps even more significantly, omniscience deadens us to the creative potential of the space of pedagogy where meanings are negotiated and where transformation occurs in the space between speaking subjects. I do not want to suggest, however, that the fantasy of omnipotence, which lends coherence to the collective story of feminism described by Grosz and which may also be at work in Tanis' narrative, can or should be exchanged for a more "reality-proof" version. Indeed, when it comes to imagining a different future for women, fantasy—conscious and unconscious, collective and singular—plays an important role. Ethel Person (1995) offers the following description of the important relations between fantasy and world-making:

> Though early psychoanalytic formulations viewed fantasy as primarily providing substitute gratification, a retreat from the external world, fantasy in fact plays a major role in building that world, in guiding the choices and adaptations we make and the relationships we form. Fantasies are among the most powerful of the catalysts that infuse and organize our lives....In turn, our experiences, and the myths and stories of the culture in which we live, shape our fantasies. Moreover, fantasy...is one

> of the crucibles in which those myths and stories are forged, and is thus a key element in cultural evolution and change. (1)

The problem is not our need for fantasies but rather our reluctance to admit our collusion in the spinning of fantasies that props up our view of the world and that which is then set in motion in social relations. By dismissing Tanis' story as having relevance for my study, I was able to hold onto my own contradictory belief that feminist discourse was a system of representation and that it was capable of telling the truth about my life. This was the traumatic perception I could not tolerate. It was the traumatic perception that shut down the possibility of articulating interesting questions that Tanis could use, if she chose, to elaborate her narrative and perhaps even to "suffer the limits in the struggle to know" (Eigen 1986, 321).

Perhaps a similar traumatic perception haunts the emancipatory commitments of critical educational research on resistance. These commitments seem to require a belief that better pedagogical practices and conditions of learning will enhance the "good stories" of resistance and act as a cure for the "bad stories." However, as my reading of Tanis' narrative suggests, the circulations of psychic resistance render the sharp distinction between good and bad stories more difficult to support. Research that relies on sociological resistance theories cannot account for the dynamics of this other resistance.

My own attachment to these meanings of resistance led me initially to reject Tanis' story as having nothing to do with resistance. I was still very invested in seeing resistance as a subject's response to the social world (in this case, the larger social world of gender inequality and the microsocial of the feminist classroom). But in order to see resistance this way, I also had to maintain a belief in the subject in charge of herself. This is the subject we have grown accustomed to meeting in critical educational research accounts. Resistance, read through the fiction of such a subject, implies opposition, but what must be opposed is constituted as an external force. These external forces reduce conflict to the effects of the social bearing down on the individual and contradiction to the effect of competing ideologies.

When we begin, however, with the split subject of psychoanalytic theory, we discover new forms of conflict and contradiction that do not reconcile easily with forms of resistance centered by sociological theories of the subject. These new forms of conflict and contradiction are quite particular to the individual, and they require us to consider the complicated ways in which learning must take a detour through psychic resistance. These insights suggest that we need to pay close attention, in our classrooms as well as in the research stories we listen to, to the curious and tiny ways that psychic resistance presents itself in the guise of narrative coherence. By reading Tanis' story as a story of resistance, I am not suggesting that she resists feminism. On the contrary, the narrative she produces owes its coherence to feminist categories and concepts. What this reading might allow is consideration of what these coherent narratives render unthinkable. It might also allow us to think of resistance as a very complex category that is overburdened with psychic as well as political meanings, investments, and effects. On this more complex view, resistance remains on the side of agency, but agency itself must be rethought to include its own otherness and that which it resists in the name of resistance.

These insights also ask us to reconsider the limits of representation as we interpret research stories. The methodological claims I make here reconstitute the problem of representing others—fairly, accurately, ethically—to the problem of self-representation. If our narratives of self-representation fail to represent ourselves to ourselves but, instead, represent the impossible desire to see ourselves, we must ask how this impossible desire plays itself out twice in research accounts—once in the self-narratives research participants present us with and again in the stories we tell about these narratives. More often than not, educational research wishes to be a discourse that learns from practice in order to transform it. If, however, we think of research as occupying that creative and dialogic space that is incommensurable with either theory or practice, we might become curious about the dynamics of learning and identity performance in research. The value of our research accounts may not lie in their capacity to represent others and their responses to our pedagogical efforts. Rather, their value may lie in what we are able to learn from these responses about the conditions of learning we want to create for our students and ourselves. Where the goal of psychoanalysis is the construction of a personal past for the analysand that can admit and engage the unconscious intrusions of the past into the present, the goal of educational research might include the construction of a theoretical/pedagogical past that can admit its own ambivalence, rigidities, and, most important, its own interminability. We might, in other words, understand our interpretative narratives as psychic events.

Chapter Four

Love Stories: Cinematic Lures and Identification from Afar

The psychoanalytic subject is an effect of its libidinal ties to others. From these ties or processes of identifications begins the work of identity. Feminist theorists' recent elaborations on Freud's work on identificatory processes have complicated our understanding of how identity makes and remakes itself in an ongoing process of relationality.[1] Psychoanalytic theory is not, however, known for taking an optimistic view of the capacity of individuals to effect their psychic transformations through larger social efforts to reduce, if not eliminate, the crippling effects of subordination and domination. Cornelius Castoriadis' (1994) definition of the Ego helps us to pinpoint the problem:

> The Ego is largely a social fabrication; it is designed to function in a given social setting and to preserve, continue and reproduce this setting, that is, the institutions which created it. These institutions are thus maintained not so much through violence and explicit coercion as through their internalization by the individuals in whose fabrication they participate. (7)

It appears that the Ego, while neither given in advance nor static, is better suited to the work of conserving than it is to transforming radically its institutional roots. Still, it is worth asking, as Castoriadis does, "[h]as psychoanalysis nothing to do with the western emancipatory movement? Is the work directed towards the knowledge of the unconscious and the transformation of the human subject totally unrelated to the question of freedom...?" (2). These are difficult questions, but Castoriadis offers a small sketch to help us. He begins with Freud's well-known insistence that pedagogy, psychoanalysis, and politics are the three impossible professions. Their impossibility, Castoriadis argues, lies not so much with the fact that they are all implicated in practices that have as their goal the changing of human beings. After all, the changing of human beings begins at the beginning of life and is inextricably bound up with the processes of becoming social subjects. In other words, what we call the development of an individual relies upon social interaction, and social interaction is informed by the larger realm of the social, the historical, and the cultural.

The deep problem identified by Castoriadis is that, at the very center of ethical psychoanalytic and pedagogical practice, one encounters a thorny paradox: one must attempt to produce autonomous human beings (that is, individuals who are "capable of self-reflexive activity and deliberation") using an autonomy that does not yet exist and that is mitigated by the prior demand that individuals "absorb and internalize existing institutions" (7). The problem for politics is similar but moves from an interest in the individual to an interest in the collective: the institution of what Castoriadis calls an autonomous society (one that creates its own laws, knows that it does so, and can use its radical imaginary to change its institutions on the basis of deliberation and reflection) requires autonomous individuals. The project of autonomy, whether individually or collectively undertaken, is akin to the notion of "praxis," and it is characterized by the frustrations of its own interminability as well as the inevitability of individual and collective delays, detours, and reversals. It is not equivalent to "praxis," however, because the activities of self-reflexivity and deliberation must confront, not only the reproductive pull of social institutions but also the curious and persistent demands of the unconscious.

Kaja Silverman's *The Threshold of the Visible World* is a thoughtful and theoretically nuanced meditation on our capacity to dream the dream of autonomous subjects. Her critical engagement with psychoanalytic theories of identification has implications for both pedagogy and politics. In terms of pedagogy, her study takes us in the direction of conceptualizing learning as a psychic process or what Shoshana Felman (1987) has called "self-subversive self-reflection" (90). Implied in this notion of learning are the study, elaboration, and unlearning of psychic investments—a re-education of the Ego involving both its conscious and unconscious dimensions. In terms of politics, Silverman explores the potential for cinema and photography to create conditions of possibility that invite audience participation in the risk of the self that such an activity entails.

The text, which takes its title from Lacan's (1977) famous essay on the mirror stage, relies upon but also substantially reworks his insistence upon the significance of the infant's apprehension of its literal reflection in the mirror for the establishment and subsequent development of its Ego. It is comprised of three chapters focusing on the productivity of the Ego (the threshold) and three focusing on the productivity of cultural practices of representation (the visible world). This division is largely one of emphasis as the Ego and the visible world require each other. Early on in the text, Silverman situates her project in an examination of her own discomfort when she is forced to pass, on her way to work at UC Berkeley, crowds of homeless people. "Each time I do so," she writes, "I am overcome with irrational panic" (26).

Initially, she understands this panic in terms of the tension between the imperative to give money and the impossibility of either satisfying the demand or making rational choices about who should receive small gifts of change. However, when Silverman recognizes that she "studiously avoids looking at the homeless people" (26), she begins to understand her dilemma as one that is more specular than economic:

> What I feel myself being asked to do, and what I resist with every fibre of my being, is to locate myself within bodies which would, quite simply, be ruinous of my middle-class self—within bodies that are calloused from sleeping on the pavement, chapped from their exposure to sun and rain, and grimy from weeks without access to a shower, and which consequently make no claim to what, within our culture, passes for "ideality." (26)

After some time has passed, she comes to an even deeper understanding of the stakes of this difficult self-knowledge:

> (...) I find it difficult but not impossible to identify with the structural position of homelessness, since I imagine that in such a situation I would still coincide with that corporeal fiction which I call "me." But the homeless people on Telegraph Avenue dispel this comforting fiction; they show me that, if homeless, I would no longer precisely be "myself." And rather than acceding to this politically imperative self-estrangement, I automatically avert my eyes. (26)

This story is useful because it demonstrates the movements of self-reflexive self-subversive activity. Silverman's shift in her analysis recalls the distinction Freud (1919a) makes when he talks about the difference between learning something *about* psychoanalysis and learning something *from* it (173). What Silverman "learns" has little to do with the knowledge that homeless people are not the architects of their economic condition. Rather, it concerns her acknowledgment of her psychic investment in her own identity as middle class. Identity, however, refers less to what it means to assert a social location, as in the utterance "I am middle class," than it refers to the feeling of occupying a middle-class body—a corporeal fiction. The narrative she tells traces the psychic distress of the Ego in the face of a demand to reconstitute its bodily boundaries. This demand becomes intelligible as a demand in the shift that Silverman articulates between the risk of identifying with a structural position and the risk of identifying with the actual bodies of homeless individuals.

Silverman draws our attention to two key dynamics with this story. The first concerns the role of affect in processes of identification. In this narrative, the affective response is one of panic, but we can easily imagine contexts that produce other responses. Consider, for example, the deep pleasure we feel when our identificatory gaze returns our bodily boundaries intact and, indeed, strengthened by the encounter. Left unexamined, neither the experience of pleasure nor the experience of "panic" effects learning. Both, however, hold potential to become the grounds of learning if we can conceive of learning as beginning with insight into our psychic investments. Silverman is interested primarily in learning to make pleasurable identifications from specular encounters with bodies that are historically marked negatively in social and cultural terms. This is the subject of the second dynamic.

Here, her narrative exposes the relationship between bodies marked by broader forms of cultural disdain and the not-so-private boundaries of her "identitary-ensemblist" (Castoriadis 1994, 3) logic. When this logic begins to break down, its force is such that one's very sense of self is severely compromised and threatened. The danger that Silverman feels and tries to ward off concerns the failure of her identity to assert itself as belonging to itself. Somewhat counterintuitively, Silverman's "crisis" does not occur because she *cannot* identify with homeless people; it occurs because she has actually come too close to identifying with them, and this proximity reveals to her the abjected limits of her own subjective position.[2] A dilemma emerges here, and it forms the core of Silverman's meditations on psychoanalytic theory and representational practices: acceding to self-estrangement may be politically imperative if the difference of the other is to be legitimated, but self-estrangement may be experienced as a profound threat that sets in motion unconscious defense mechanisms.

The Education and Re-Education of the Bodily Ego

Silverman's study centers the exploration of the conditions under which self-estrangement might be coaxed into the more productive work of elaborating and enlarging the Ego. She begins with Freud's assertion that the Ego is, "first and foremost, a bodily ego; it is not merely a surface entity, but is itself the projection of a surface"[3] (1). Simply put, the surface of the self is not there, waiting to be fully experienced by the developing individual; it is, rather, more like a work of art that comes into being as the effects of touching and being touched, seeing and being seen. Like Castoriadis and others who insist that psychoanalysis does have something to say to and about the question of freedom, Silverman considers the Ego's capacity to distinguish between what belongs to itself and what belongs to another Ego as crucial to learning to tolerate and, indeed, to take pleasure in the other's enjoyment of her/his bodily Ego.

At the same time, however, Silverman is suspicious of what she calls the "popular notion of the mobile subject, open to an infinitude of contradictory identifications" (2). The Ego, as she understands it, is much less tractable than such theories would have us believe. Implicit in her critique is a need to rethink feminist, anti-racist, and neo-Marxist pedagogical narratives that rely upon role models, the correction of stereotypes, and counterhegemonic knowledge to change learners unproblematically. These pedagogical theories have made significant contributions to our understandings of how representational practices and knowledge are organized by normative imperatives and used to prop up discriminatory practices. We seem to be less clear about the complicated ways in which people attach or do not attach to knowledge and how these attachments turn into actions. When Silverman names her response to homeless people as "irrational panic," she echoes a concern raised in recent writing about students' engagements with counter-hegemonic knowledge and consciousness-raising strategies that examines students' refusals of knowledge which ostensibly serves their interests.

While resistance is frequently conceptualized as a problem of the obduracy of "internalized oppression" or its opposite term, "internalized privilege," educators have become increasingly aware of the limitations of those strategies named above to help students gain insight into their structures of meaning-making practices.[4] Silverman's elaboration of the bodily Ego and its reliance upon unconscious processes of identification contributes to a growing interest in what psychic investments have to do with learning and not learning.[5] When learning is conceived as a psychic event, resistance to knowledge is conceptualized as the very grounds of possibility for learning rather than as an impediment to it. In the face of "irrational panic," one must choose between turning away and turning toward the source of the panic—the Ego.

Silverman's choice is clear, and the route she traces begins with the concept of love. In fact, love is the central organizing theme of this text. Her emphasis on love and the Ego boundaries it effects and helps to dissolve may come as a surprise to many readers. For many of us working in the field of education, the spectre of love in that place where politics and pedagogy intersect may usher in images of excesses of power that feminist and anti-racist scholars have been at such pains to apprise us of over the past twenty years. Or it may remind us of well-meaning but naive notions of care of and for the other that forget the specificity of the other. These two kinds of love—which may be two sides of the same narcissistic coin—do figure as a problem in Silverman's text, but the theoretical and aesthetic framework she develops insists upon tying love to conceptual work: where idealizing love exists, so also exists an idea. However, idealization is largely an unconscious process. For this reason, the ideas that cling to idealization and the idealization that clings to ideas must be teased out, articulated, and reflected upon. In other words, unconscious processes of idealization and de-idealization must be rendered consciously if their political significance is to be grasped. While Silverman believes that political cinema might profit from different ways of thinking about the role love plays in the realm of the political, she also emphasizes the persistence of a gap between psychic relations and the intentions of cultural representations. This gap, it seems to me, is a site of pedagogy.

For Silverman and, indeed, for Freud, idealizing love is the name given to those early object relations that provide the structure for subsequent identificatory bonds. As such, loving and being beloved are requisites for coming into being as a social subject. At the same time, however, love also represents a kind of state of emergency for the emerging subject, serving as a constant reminder of the fact that we are not the omnipotent authors of our existence and that love can be withdrawn or lost. I return below to Silverman's discussion of idealizing love, but here it might be useful to establish why this concept holds the importance it does in a study of social relations at the level of the collective. Silverman explains,

> (...) those of us writing deconstructively about gender, race, class, and other forms of "difference" have made a serious strategic mistake. We have consistently argued against idealization, that psychic activity at the heart of love, rather than imagining the new uses to which it might be put. In so doing, we have left the existing system of ideals unchallenged and overlooked a crucial component in the identificatory process. (2)

Cultural theorists have argued against idealization, in part, because of the understanding, so crucial to early critical and feminist film theory, that this process has figured prominently in the ways in which dominant forms of cultural representation provoke identification with subject positions already organized to serve certain interests. Indeed, Silverman acknowledges that her earlier work theorizes cinematic identification largely "in terms of the subject's insertion into a normative position"[6] (85). We can attribute a second difficulty to the appropriations of psychoanalytic theorizing that have been brought to bear on the study of cultural practices of representation. The work of Lacan, well known for its assault on post-Freudian formulations of the

Ego as a self-determining agent, has been invaluable to cultural critiques' understanding of the relationship between subjectivity and representation. Here, the anxious desire for representation to fill the gap between presence and being has been linked to a notion of identification characterized primarily as an incorporative assault on the other in an effort to secure the elusive sensation of a coherent and unified bodily Ego.[7]

Silverman's arguments challenge both of these concerns even as they remain important developments in our understanding, on the one hand, of normative representational practices and, on the other hand, those dimensions of idealization that inhibit the expansion of our libidinal attachments. If idealization is a necessary psychic process, she reasons, then the identificatory "lure" of cinema may be its most valuable asset because it "represents the potential for a spectatorial self-estrangement" (85). The films and photographs she reads in conjunction with her exploration of how spectatorial self-estrangement can be achieved demonstrate that such works of art already exist. Silverman focuses on the political potential of "beauty" read through cinematic strategies that "dismantle the illusory unity of the body schema, and situate the visual imago insistently outside, where it can be renegotiated" (93). The development of new cinematic strategies, as well as the recognition of the richness of those already in existence, depends, in the first instance, upon an elaboration of a theory of identification that exceeds and complicates the incorporative model.

Silverman's approach follows that of her other works of film theory[8] by engaging with Lacanian theory, and here she provides readers who are unfamiliar with his notoriously difficult work with a lucid introduction to some of his key concepts. She also draws upon other psychoanalytic theorists and cultural critics to imagine a subject whose capacity to idealize can combine with a susceptibility to culture to work against the logic of incorporation and, at the same time, *toward* the idealization of socially repudiated bodies. Here is how Silverman describes the textual moves most central to her study:

> Idealization is...a crucial political tool, which can give us access to a whole range of new psychic relations. However, we cannot decide that we will henceforth idealize differently; that activity is primarily unconscious, and for the most part textually steered. We consequently need aesthetic works which will make it possible for us to idealize, and, so, to identify with bodies we would otherwise repudiate. (2)

Henri Wallon's (1934) study of infants' response to a mirror plays a central role in re-evaluating Lacan's notion of the founding of the Ego in the mirror stage and allows Silverman to make a distinction between identificatory processes ruled by an externalizing logic, which holds the potential for recognizing another as a subject, and those ruled by an internalizing logic, which leans toward the tendency to incorporate and, hence (metaphorically), destroy the other. What is emphasized in Lacan's account of the mirror stage is the notion that the infant's apprehension of "self" is installed at the moment of self-recognition in the image reflected by the mirror. This is, of course, also a misrecognition, and we are familiar with Lacan's insistence that this misrecognition brings into being the split subject.

Wallon theorizes a process that is less instantaneous. Moreover, he argues that self-recognition is a culminating rather than inaugurating event. He suggests that the infant perceives its image in the mirror as something both connected to but also separate from itself. For Wallon, in order for the "self" to be apprehended as such, two components must be laboriously brought together. One component is what he calls the exteroceptive Ego, that is, the image of the self in the mirror. The second component he calls the proprioceptive Ego, and this refers to the sense of the self as a material occupant in space. The significant difference between Lacan's account of the mirror stage and Wallon's is that the latter suggests a developing Ego that can tolerate, at least initially, some degree of incoherence or disunity between these disparate parts. Silverman draws several conclusions from her study of Wallon and other theorists of early identificatory processes. She becomes curious about the effects of various cultural imperatives, whether these lean towards papering over that gap through psychic mechanisms of disavowal and repudiation or towards heightening the unpleasurable ways the gap between the body one occupies and normative ideals produce particularized experiences of psychic dilemmas. However, Silverman is also interested in the productive and creative potential of this revised understanding of the mirror stage. She suggests that perceiving one's reflection in the mirror constitutes "identity-at-a-distance," which she defines as a corporeal and specular otherness that also seems to be within the bodily Ego.

This notion of the development of a sense of self as simultaneously apprehended from within and "at-a-distance" creates more potential than Lacan seems to permit for the Ego to recognize another subject as separate from itself. This is crucial for Silverman's assertions that a politically productive relation to bodily otherness requires a process of identification that is exteriorizing rather than interiorizing. This other subject, apprehended both near and at a distance, can be idealized as "good" or "beautiful" even if it does not possess the features that would make it a good candidate for affirming and elaborating the ideal Ego. Moreover, when the logic of identification proceeds along a trajectory of exteriorization, the image that is reflected back to the viewer is not assimilated to the self and thus retains the features of its own corporeal singularity.

Silverman does not overlook the dangers of idealizing forms of love that exalt the object. Indeed, much of the first section of the book is devoted to a thorough study of the different forms idealization can take and how these forms enhance or diminish the possibility of making productive use of identity-at-a-distance to facilitate new psychic relations. Where other theorists have explored the radical implications of rethinking psychical relations in terms of the cultural imperatives of heterosexuality that enforce, albeit often unsuccessfully, the distinction between same-sex identifications and object-choice identifications,[9] Silverman addresses a range of processes of idealization in relation to the subject's sense of its corporeal boundaries. This does not mean that sexual love does not figure in her scheme. Rather, Silverman's emphasis on the ways in which ideal images play a role in facilitating relations to all love objects is important precisely because it creates a space for theorizing love as a gift that can be bestowed on identities who are idealized from afar and, hence, in relations that locate the desires of wanting to be or wanting to have the other within a broader range of social markers of idealization and de-idealization.

These new spaces allow for a rethinking of the familiar injunction in education to love the other as you love yourself. The experience of self-love, which Silverman defines as "those rare occasions when we imaginarily coincide with the ideal image which we usually worship from afar" (39), may be the most intensely pleasurable form of love we have access to. It is, nevertheless, a poor model for facilitating new psychic relations with socially denigrated bodies for several reasons. One important observation that Silverman offers is that one's ideal image typically derives from normative ideals—a factor not lost on mainstream film industries.

More than this, however, our attempts to approximate our ideal image do tend to follow the logic of incorporation. To the extent that these attempts are successful, we love ourselves at the expense of the world and its inhabitants. The object is incorporated and, hence, ceases to exist in its own right. To the extent that such attempts are unsuccessful, the failure to approximate the wished-for wholeness that we attribute to the object plunges us into feelings of insufficiency, discordance, and disarray. The fantasy of the object's wholeness, in the face of our own distance from it, provokes our murderous rivalry with the object. Ulrike Ottinger's (1979) *Bildnis einer Trinkerin (Ticket of No Return)* examines one woman's pathological obsession with a mirror reflection of idealized femininity. Silverman reads against the feminist grain of interpreting the film as the logical outcome of our society's insistence upon collapsing women with their image. She emphasizes instead the terrible consequences of the protagonist's inability to accept her exteriority to the idealizing image of femininity.

Idealization, if it is to become a tool for political cinema, must take the form of enhancing, not self-love but rather loving relations with others. In order for ideal images to foster loving identifications, two conditions must be met. Silverman argues that "ideality can only serve these vital functions when it is bestowed at the greatest possible distance from the self, and when that bestowal is active rather than passive" (41). In order to avoid the "either you or me" logic of self-love identifications, the subject must be encouraged to shift from a preoccupation with seeking ideality that affirms its sense of self to a preoccupation with bestowing ideality on an other. The notion of identity-at-a-distance, theorized above as integral to the early stages of the formation of the bodily Ego, plays a central role in this process. These infantile processes are played out unconsciously, prior to the child's entry into the symbolic realm of language, and within the confines of the family romance. The subsequent elaboration of identity-at-a-distance into the bestowal of the active gift of love is a project of the fully social subject.

The specular relation so central to the infant's constitution of a bodily Ego in the mirror stage acts as a prototype for further development. For Lacan, the mirror gives way to the "screen," which represents the site of the Ego's further elaboration as a social subject. And, much in the same way that the infant's (mis)recognition in the mirror is facilitated by another person, usually the mother, one's visual identity as a social subject is facilitated by the "gaze." Identification, then, must be understood as a three-way, rather than a two-way, transaction that requires symbolic ratification:

> In order to emerge within the field of vision, the subject must not only align him-or herself identificatorily with the screen, but must also be apprehended in that guise by the gaze. (18)

While symbolic ratifications are historically and culturally constituted, contested and reformulated, we can no more choose how we are apprehended visually than we can "conjure" a screen that we like better. Silverman offers two ways out of this bind:

> We can struggle at a collective level to transform the existing (screen). Alternatively, we can try at an individual level to substitute another image for the one through which we are conventionally seen, or, to deform or reromanticize the normative image. (19)

The film that exemplifies for Silverman the first alternative is Isaac Julien's *Looking for Langston*. According to Silverman, Julian has created an imagistic world that cannot be entered without the audience's willing and self-conscious participation in a process of radical self-estrangement. Her reading, which is as lush as the film itself, examines the narrative and cinematic structures that Julien uses to simultaneously idealize the bodies of black gay men and insist upon their radical singularity. They become both subjects and objects of desire in ways that resist assimilation into the fantasies of the dominant white culture. In the final chapter of the book, Cindy Sherman's *Untitled Film Stills* becomes the focus of an elaborate study of the screen against which white women in our culture are "given-to-be-seen." In this example of the second alternative, Sherman's photographs draw attention to the desire of the model to be photographed so as to ensure that she is "seen" in terms that seek to affirm her structures of self-idealization even as they also heighten the viewer's awareness of the "framing" of the poses and, hence, of the normalizing particularities of the desire itself.

In all of the interpretive studies she offers to move her theoretical gestures along, Silverman interweaves her analysis of the formal qualities of the still and moving camera with a discussion of the complex interplay between the eye of the individual and the eye of the camera. I have focused my discussion on the processes of identification that comprise the first half of the book because it is these dynamics that are most directly implicated in pedagogical practices. Silverman's insistence that idealization is both necessary to human existence and subject to the repetitive "lure" of dominant representational practices raises new questions about what is at stake when students "love" or "hate" the texts, visual or print, that we offer as ways into the lived experience of marginalized identities. As Teresa Brennan (1989) suggests, learning occurs in the fault lines of idealizing pleasures and prohibitions:

> We can postulate that an ego-ideal identification with feminism in the form of a person, people, or a body of writing, suspends the ego-ideal's existing prohibitions, that it permits different thinking. For when the ego identifies itself with a social other, it is permeable to the wish, will or ideas of that other. (10)

Pedagogy uses the creative play between prior prohibitions and their suspension. When learning is conceptualized as a linear process based on rational judgment, too easily forgotten are the traumas of confronting, losing, and refinding psychic investments that accrue to the learner. However, also forgotten are the Ego's tendencies to lay down new prohibitions at the very site of these creative acts. Identity-at-a-distance introduces an important construct for pedagogy because it highlights the psychic importance of idealization for learning while also drawing attention to its illusory nature. That is, it opens the possibility of acknowledging that idealization is not the same thing as identity and that the idealized other exists for her- or himself.

If ideality is to be conferred at-a-distance, students need opportunities to engage with materials that call attention to—even as they disrupt—identificatory practices that are aligned with normative practices. Silverman's study suggests that imaginative works may play a more important role than we are accustomed to believing in creating the conditions for learning about social hatreds and discriminations. Art that works at the level of fantasy encourages the elaboration and enlargement of the Ego's libidinal attachments. Indeed, the political value of such works may lie more in their structures of fantasy than in their capacity to "tell the truth" or maintain the fiction of "realistic" representation. Knowledge about social difference may only begin to matter to how we choose to act in the world when it is accompanied or even preceded by the beautiful fiction of the world as if it already were otherwise.

Notes

1. See, for instance, Judith Butler 1993 and Diana Fuss 1995.

2. For a discussion of the complex processes of sexual identifications that require both "positive" identification with a sexual position and a "negative" identification with that position's repudiated other, see Judith Butler 1993.

3. The quotation is taken from Freud's essay, "The Ego and the Id," 1923.

4. See Laurie Finke 1993; Patti Lather 1991; Magda Lewis 1990; Kathleen Martindale 1992; Cameron McCarthy & Warren Crichlow (eds.) 1993.

5. See Deborah Britzman 1995b; Shoshana Felman 1987; Judith Robertson 1997; Sharon Todd (ed.) 1997.

6. Here Silverman refers to *The Subject of Semiotics*, 1983.

7. See, for instance, Peggy Phelan 1993.

8. In addition to *The Subject of Semiotics*, see *The Acoustic Mirror: The Female Voice in Psychoanalysis and Cinema* (1988) and *Male Subjectivity at the Margins* (1992).

9. See, for instance, Mikkel Borch-Jacobsen 1994 and Jessica Benjamin 1995.

Chapter Five

Hide and Seek: The Play of the Personal in Education

It is a joy to be hidden but disaster not to be found.
—D.W. Winnicott, *Communicating and Not Communicating*

The popular children's pastime of hide and seek provides D.W. Winnicott with a metaphor for the serious though also creative and ambivalent work of communication. Near the end of his life, he explores the subject of communication from an odd vantage: "the right not to communicate" (1965, 179). Surprised by this idea, he writes, "this was a protest from the core of me to the frightening fantasy of being infinitely exploited" (179). The emergence of this frightening fantasy complicates Winnicott's study of dependence in two kinds of relationships—mother/child and analyst/analysand. His insistence that there exists, at the very core of the individual, a permanently isolated and secret self, opens the underside of object-relations theory. While this theory does place a premium upon the collaborative role of others in the work of self-formation, there is something of a protest that can trail the pleasures of communication. The infant's need to communicate and to use the communicative efforts of others as the grounds of development into an individual who can "feel real" is countered by the equally pressing need to defend against communication with the secret self. Communication itself is experienced as an urgent game of hide and seek.

This paradoxical claim startles our common-sense understandings about the psychoanalytic enterprise as a talking cure. We are likely to be familiar with the notion that the most secret aspect of ourselves resides in the unconscious, that it speaks (in dreams, slips of the tongue), and that our suffering from inner conflict can be attenuated, though never completely resolved, by learning the truth of our unconscious selves. The idea that communication with the secret self is experienced as profoundly exploitative poses new challenges to psychoanalysts for whom the analysand's refusal of analytic interpretations continues to be construed primarily as resistance to be worked through. It is also a challenge to educators who value the personal as the grounds of teaching and learning. In Winnicott's view, the refusal of the analyst's interpretation signals intrusive communication that must be withdrawn immediately. He makes a distinction between interpretations that can be used by patients to "make good their lives" (Phillips 1998, 65) and those experienced as intrusive to the secret self. The analyst's specialized knowledge must be held in abeyance as he waits for clues from the patient that express need. These different values on the uses of interpreting the personal raise new questions for educators.

Finding and making things matter and inventing satisfying stories to explain what we care about to ourselves and others is nothing more and nothing less than the work of living and of learning. It is curious work, highly idiosyncratic, on the one hand, and profoundly shaped by collective cultural imperatives, on the other. It is uneven in its development, sometimes eagerly pursued; at other times its movement is barely perceptible. At its most tragic, such appetite may be lost or so deeply mislaid or mistrusted that it feels lost. Winnicott's notion of an isolated and secret self along with his insistence upon the individual's right and need to resist the analyst's interpretations create a puzzle for psychoanalysts, who are among those professionals sought out when life fails to feel satisfying. In Winnicott's work we can identify pieces of this puzzle that I shall explore in relation to some contemporary discussions of "the personal" in educational research. Here is one way of naming the puzzle: one must learn how to do this work of sustaining an appetite for life, but it cannot be taught. The material of the work, the stories themselves, can be transformed over time, but they cannot be exchanged (Felman 1987). However enjoyment of them can be enhanced when they can be engaged with by others. We might say that stories, yours and mine, can be used in this work of sustaining appetite for life, but just how we approach stories raises difficult ethical, methodological, and epistemological questions. Our entry into the social world, where we undertake the strange work of inventing ourselves as a story, is always haunted by loss. Our stories are paid for by substituting some of our most deeply felt desires and wishes for more socially acceptable ones that we must come to love dearly if we are to gain a sufficient measure of satisfaction from and for the work of living. For Freud, this is experienced as a tension between id-gratification of instinctual drives and ego-gratification born of social endeavors, ultimately expressed as the conflict between two instincts, the life drive (Eros) and the death drive (Thanatos). For Winnicott, it is experienced as a tension between compliance and "feeling real" and expressed as "the conflict between two trends, to communicate and to hide" (Phillips 1988, 151). The question for Winnicott is "how to be isolated without having to be insulated" (1965, 187).

Winnicott's question has resonance for educators who recognize the loneliness of teaching (Britzman 1998; Knoblock & Goldstein 1971) and the difficulty of sustaining an appetite for life as a teacher in times of shrinking resources and expanding, often contradictory, demands. Recent discussions in educational research elaborate the category of the personal in an attempt to illuminate how teachers and students make good their lives in the intimate space of the classroom and in the less intimate space of the institutions that organize the work of the teacher. I shall revisit some of the debates surrounding this literature and consider what Winnicott offers as an alternative way of thinking about these dilemmas. I begin with a story that describes a moment when the demand for the personal was experienced as breaching rather than bridging the space between life inside and life outside the classroom. It is this story that has provoked me to ponder the inexpressible qualities of the personal and then what dilemmas this category poses for research and pedagogy.

During an informal conversation with a beginning teacher, she focused her uneasiness on new guidelines for teaching French-as-a-second language in her region's elementary schools. The advice given for the first meeting with students surprised and troubled her. She was advised to take photographs of herself and her family members into the class to use as props for the introduction of the teacher and the curriculum. Students were also encouraged to bring along samples from their own family albums to complete the circle of introductions. The lesson, simple, apparently benign, and probably familiar in its basic structure to many who spend time in classrooms, enacts some taken-for-granted ideas about how one tradition within the field of education understands teacher identity, students' needs and the relational webs of curriculum, student learning and pedagogical practice. Much can be teased out of this example that resonates with assumptions about the role and qualities of the personal in teaching and learning. This teacher encountered these assumptions in her own teacher education, where she learned to be curious about what children come to school already knowing and create lessons using the base of lived experience to encourage exploration of the unknown. Indeed, part of her uneasiness about this particular lesson was rooted in what she saw as a conflict within the demands of the lesson. How, she wondered, could we assume that bringing in family photos posed no emotional or material problems for children or their caregivers?

She was also bothered by the demand that the teacher use her private life to prop up a lesson. She recognized that some teachers' personal lives must be kept private because they do not map neatly on to dominant assumptions about who teachers can be, given the demands that they serve as role models for children. We played with images that we thought would be unacceptable: nudist teachers on a family outing, same-sex couples, even one-parent families evoked the presence of a gap between the demand and its execution. There was still something more—something she could not quite put her finger on. She could only say, "There is something creepy about this." How might our assumptions about what we need to *know about* our students in order to teach them (and conversely, what they need to *know about us* in order to learn from us) give us the creeps? What is creepy about a theory of language that centers the social real (authentically captured in a photograph) as both a means and an end to learning how language works and how we become participants in linguistic world-making? What, in other words, might we learn if we pay attention to the affective quality of this teacher's response to the demand to use the personal in her pedagogical efforts?

The paradoxical desires of hiding and being discovered that so concerned Winnicott suggest that revealing and concealing what we take to be personal about the work of teaching turn on something very complex. The familiar oppositions between public and private and between the individual and the systemic may not allow such complexity to be noticed. Who has not played hide and seek, only to experience the giddy pleasure of the game spoiled when too little or too much time has passed between finding the perfect hiding place and being (re)discovered? The perfect hiding place needs to be settled into, and yet, if occupied too long, becomes dark and lonely, even frightening. A similar dynamic structures our experiences with the personal when it crops up in the classroom or when it is posed as a category for educational research into teaching. Perhaps we should not be surprised when we experience telling (or showing) the details of our personal lives, not as illuminating the self for another but as a threat to the integrity of the self.

For Winnicott, the dangers and pleasures of play are central to healthy development (1971a). Taking pleasure in the play and recovering from its breakdowns constitute the movements of developmental achievement for the infant. What distinguishes Winnicott's ideas about play from other developmental theories (and from the French lesson) is his understanding that play occurs in an area of life that *is in between* reality and fantasy. Play belongs solely to neither realm of experience. Winnicott calls this intermediate space the transitional space. The infant's early encounters with this space are mediated by the use of a transitional object (1992c). A transitional object represents for the baby the first Not-Me object. This object is characterized by a paradox: it exists in the world, *and* it is brought into existence by the infant. The play between subjectively creating and finding the object constitutes the performative work of coming-into-being of the child, who must move from absolute dependence to relative dependence to disillusionment. Winnicott describes disillusionment as the capacity to notice and tolerate that one has not, in fact, created the object but has encountered it. Its existence as separate from the child confronts the child with a world that is outside the realm of its control: this, according to Winnicott, comes as a big shock. Much of his work concerns the difficulty of relating "subjective reality to shared reality which can be objectively perceived" (Phillips 1988, 117). The transitional object "bridges for the child what might seem, without this connection, to be two incompatible worlds" (Phillips, 118).

The ability to tolerate the persistence of discontinuities between subjective reality and shared reality is not merely a phase-specific mode of adaptation to reality that one grows out of as beloved objects are set aside and untenable theories about how the world works are abandoned in favor of more collective visions that can then be challenged on purely rational grounds. Rather, the intermediate area of experiencing inner reality and external life together remains important throughout our lives. As Adam Phillips notes,

> (...) development through the use of Transitional Phenomena was not for Winnicott, as it was for Freud, a process of cumulative disillusionment; it was not a growing capacity for mourning, but a growing capacity to tolerate the continual and increasingly sophisticated illusionment-disillusionment-re-illusionment process throughout the life-cycle. (1988, 121)

Winnicott's interest in our use of objects and the persistence of tensions between subjective or inner reality and shared or outer reality allowed him to consider the analytic setting as a transitional space for "a highly specialized form of playing in the service of communicating with oneself and others" (1971a, 48). Also developing directly out of play is a different kind of transitional space he calls "cultural experience." He uses this concept to talk about the movements between inner and outer reality that occur in our experience with all kinds of knowledge. His interest is less in what we learn from our encounters with knowledge about the world; rather, he is curious about what we use knowledge to do. Here, too, we play at hiding and being found.

The Use of the Personal

What do we use the personal to do? I have hinted at two ways in which we use the personal. One way refers to the stories we tell to make good our lives. We use these stories to make sense of ourselves in ways that give meaning to our lives. A second use is evident in my conversation with the teacher, where we puzzle over the demands made upon teachers and students to use the details of their private lives as curriculum material. We use these stories to make relations with others. But some uses do feel creepy, and there is a protest when the demand to make ourselves known is felt as a violation.

Ambivalence marks the use of the personal itself. However, in educational debates, the ambivalence resides in the meaning and significance of the personal for research rather than within the personal. For advocates, personal stories about teaching and learning complicate traditional understandings in a field dominated by positivistic methods, pressures to generalize, and desires for technical solutions to tidy problems (Pinar *et al.*1995). Particulars of the perspectives of women and minority groups, previously unnoticed, provide powerful counternarratives to the official histories of education and school experience (McCarthy & Crichlow 1993; Miller 1996). Research on teacher thinking, offered as an antidote to mechanistic orientations to teaching, magnifies how the things that matter to teachers are expressed in their classroom practices (Connelly & Clandinin 1988; Elbaz 1983).

Critics worry that the use of the personal in educational research draws attention away from the structural effects of social inequalities that organize schooling (Apple 1979). More recent critiques take up poststructuralist suspicions that the narrative strategies we use to render our lives meaningful and coherent are saturated with meanings and idealizations (Convery 1999; Miller 1998; Willinsky 1989) we have inherited rather than created. While some poststructural considerations of personal narratives emphasize the ways in which the specificity of the personal fades under the logic of larger social forces, others do depict the worlds of teachers and teaching in terms of the messy and contradictory ways in which the individual past of the teacher neither maps neatly onto the present of practice nor ever becomes fully present in the strange time of classroom interactions.

Unlike the French lesson discussed earlier, that seems to assume that the public role and the private identity of the teacher can be collapsed *and* used as a conduit for the delivery of the curriculum, Britzman (1991) considers both aspects of identity as being in constant tension with one another even as each revises the other in an ongoing process of becoming. Her study of what teaching does to teachers, how meanings break down and are reworked, and how experience organizes perception rather than the other way around, rethinks how teachers learn to teach and how they learn from their teaching. There is still something more, and this has to do with what constitutes the personal in the first place. We begin to sense that the personal is something a great deal more complicated than either the developers of the French lesson or some educational researchers might be willing to admit. The personal is not merely a set of attributes that can be pointed to or named, nor is it a bank of experiences to be drawn upon unproblematically to render the world visible. Rather, the personal is constituted within a web of relations that includes relations of time (how the past works on the present) and relations with others, knowledge, and authority. The hide and seek of the personal is played out on this terrain, but its movements may exceed the force of the ideological and the institutional.

Conceding that the personal is vulnerable to the various forms of cultural imperatives that haunt classroom life and the social world still leaves an import question unanswered. How does the personal become, well, personal? Winnicott's notion of cultural experience as a transitional space suggests that it may be more useful to locate the personal not in content that reflects the world but rather as a method for observing how we experience ourselves in the world. When the personal is considered as a method of experiencing rather than as an assertion of stable experience, new possibilities emerge for considering the personal as a construct for use in world-making. These possibilities are not without paradox, dependent as they are on the strange motion of time that traverses, in unpredictable ways, illusionment-disillusionment-re-illusionment. Two different examples, one drawn from a research story and another from a story about teaching, offer insight into the work of noticing the traces of these movements.

Taking Sides: Dilemmas in Feminist Research

Leslie Bloom (1998) describes her efforts to use and come to terms with the limits of feminist research methodology in a project of writing the life histories of two feminist teachers who were well advanced in their careers. Bloom explores her disillusionment with the imperatives of feminist methodology and her insight into the ways in which such imperatives can work to shut down thinking about the complexities of women's lives and their interpersonal relationships. Within the context of the difficult work of making and sustaining a collaborative research relationship, stories emerge about how the two participants make good their lives as women and as feminists. One of these stories is an exemplary demonstration of the movement between fantasy and reality. It is a story about how one of the participants, Olivia, used her role in a high-level management position to force the company to fire a man responsible for numerous and egregious instances of sexual harassment. Upon reading her own narrative in a transcript provided by Bloom, she became curious about what this and other stories did not say:

> I had recalled the good part of several stories and failed to mention the less satisfying sides of these stories. In part this made me feel dishonest. I thought hard about

> that. I did not remember editing these stories in the telling, and I wondered why these stories emerged and not the less satisfying ones. (72)

Another version of the story reveals that Olivia had been slow to act upon women's complaints. She recalls her frustration that the women involved seemed so frozen in helplessness, forgetting how much these women depended on their jobs. For too long, it seems, she allowed herself to be persuaded by her male colleagues that the behaviors were harmless. Finally, we also learn that her investigation culminated in the removal of the man to a consulting position with an affiliated firm, a compromise that Olivia now recalls with repulsion. Bloom interprets the more complex and conflict-filled story as working against, even transcending, the conventions of the "classical story of the hero's journey" (73) that we have all inherited but which fail to account adequately for women's experiences. She also points that Olivia's "feminist heroine version of the story" rang true because it was "a story that many of us wanted, indeed, needed to hear" (85).

Bloom uses this observation to account for her own "belief" in the first version of the story and her surprise that she did not even think to question it. Her complicity takes two forms. She identified with Olivia as heroine, taking great pleasure in her ability to take the side of women and to effect a resolution that placed a priority on women's right to a safe and comfortable working environment. She also attributes some of her inattentiveness to the other inherited script at stake here, the script of feminist research methods that advise us to believe what women tell us. Perhaps these two moments of complicity belong to the same puzzle: feminist researchers have needed both to believe the stories told them by women and to hear in these stories examples of successful feminist intervention. The arena of "cultural experience" for feminism has been and continues to be an arena of the "not-yet" and the "not quite," set within a social reality not of our own making. The line between creating and finding objects is a blurred one that follows the trajectory of need before accuracy.

The difference between the two versions of Olivia's story suggests that it has become possible for the narrator to relinquish a bit of the illusion of feminist omnipotence, to find a more complex social reality, and to contemplate her own complicity and relative vulnerability in the maintenance of unequal power relations. While the research relationship did not produce Olivia's self-transformation, it did seem to create conditions that were conducive to the kind of play that Winnicott claims as characteristic of psychoanalytic communication, where created objects can be reconceived as found objects and regarded in new ways. What may be most significant about this achievement is that it was instigated by Olivia, who was able to question her own use of her story. Bloom's participation was set in motion by her surprise at her own response to the happy story and her ability to become curious about the nature of the wish that structured her initial response.

There is a belated quality both in the narratives Olivia tells and in Bloom's response. Belatedness is, for Freud, the hallmark of traumatic experience, signalling the incompleteness not just of the narrative but of the experience itself. From Winnicott's perspective, the chronology of the appearance of the two stories, along with Bloom's investment and its dispersal, represents two extremes of communication—the wish to hide and the wish to communicate—and the corresponding subjective states of illusion and disillusionment. If the first narrative represents as well as enacts the illusion that feminist intervention has the power to name and transform the conditions under which we live, it is an illusion that makes thinking and acting possible in the first place. Disillusionment, which tolerates and even enjoys interpretation, arrives on its own schedule if it is not to shatter the subject. The achievement of the capacity to tolerate disillusionment enlarges our hopes for the future and for choices because both the past and the present can be more fully experienced, and wishes can be distinguished from reality. Our capacity to think begins with our tolerance of disillusionment.

Drawing Lines: Limits of the Personal in Pedagogy

Movement between illusionment and disillusionment and the extreme poles of communication guide the practical and ethical concerns of Madeleine Grumet's pedagogy. In an essay first presented at Jane Gallop's conference, entitled "Pedagogy: The Question of the Personal," Grumet (1995) admits her ambivalence about the category of the personal even though her work has long been associated with the concept. With William Pinar (Pinar & Grumet 1976; see also Grumet 1988), she elaborates a method for using autobiography in teacher education and curriculum theory that emphasizes the difficulty of the work of self-reflection. Her discomfort was shared by other presenters and is registered in the title of the published version of presentations: *Pedagogy: The Question of Impersonation* (Gallop 1995a).

Several participants draw on notions of theatrical performance to think through their estrangement from "the personal," but Grumet may have won the prize for a performance that features her own impersonation of herself. She contemplates the Latin origins of person, *personare,* meaning "to sound through, later falling from act to object as a mask, the thing through which one sounds as in a play: dramatis personae" (37). With this obscured meaning in mind, she offers her own definition of the personal, one that wrenches the concept from the binaries with which it is so often associated. For her, the personal is "a performance, an appearance contrived for the public," and it is "these masks [that] enable us to perform the play of pedagogy" (37). Grumet introduces her pedagogical mask by showing us what she wears when she thinks, reads, and writes at home. She presents us with an old, fuzzy green bathrobe. At the conference, she hung the robe from the podium where it remained throughout her talk. The bathrobe is transformed as it makes this journey from Grumet's home to the stage:

> It is a robe I write in, not about. It is strange to see it move into the yellow letters on my screen.
>
> It is my robe, it has my smell, as I present it to you...it becomes my costume. I may never write again. (37)

It is easy to feel drawn into the personal world of Madeleine Grumet, a world which points out rather than ignores her body and her habits when she is not out in the world. However, her gesture and even the richly detailed description of robe, and her in it, signal boundaries, not the collapse between Grumet at-home and Grumet in-the-world. The robe becomes a costume when it is trotted out for public display. These boundaries and the spaces between them are the subject of her discussion of her pedagogy. Grumet describes a requirement that students in her philosophy of education course write, in typewritten form, three narratives of educational experience. Some philosophical and literary texts help students remember that their work is to fashion "representations of subjectivity for the public world" (38). The narratives, like the green robe, are costumes, not to be mistaken for the selves that narrate them. As we shall see, however, Grumet remains mindful that the narrating selves may be vulnerable, that what is too deeply personal to be interpreted may flow onto the page. Here is how Grumet describes the narratives and her engagement with them:

> Each set of three held a green world, thick with vegetation, and the only way I could make my way through it was in my green robe.
>
> Green-robed, I could crawl through their leaves, feel the rhythm of their sentences. Move to the places they skipped over. A semiotic reading, if you will. I hated entering those texts, giving up my world for theirs, but once I had migrated, I started speaking in their tongue, I became a citizen, started taking notes, started speaking back, asking questions. (39)

Grumet feels the pull of these narratives, but she also recognizes the cost to her own sense of self of entering into the green vernacular. As Grumet reads, memories of her childhood are evoked. Still in her green robe, the world she has given returns, unbidden, in the form of memories that are at once her own and deeply enmeshed with the students' writing. The boundary that separates the reading teacher from the writing students threatens to dissolve. Grumet, in order to respond to the students' narratives in ways that return them all to the world, must leave this claustrophobic hot-house.

She has developed some techniques for making this return passage. She limits her writing on the text to discreet numbers that refer the student to typed commentary on a separate page. A few comments address the text itself, but, for the most part, Grumet uses the response to invite students "to think about [their] stories and to relate them to questions about education"(44). She does not share her personal memories, nor does she ask students to account for the social causes of their experiences. Perhaps she understands that such a demand risks forcing students to distinguish much too soon between the illusion of creating and the disillusion of finding their self-representations. What she does do is provide some questions that have been raised for her by the narratives. The questions are philosophical and capacious in their reach. They act as a bridge between the narratives and the social world where teacher and students meet. Grumet recommends readings. These interpretive gestures are suggestions, gifts, perhaps, that students must decide whether or not to use and, if so, how. They are drawn from the world that Grumet loves and uses to communicate with herself and others. In response to one student's stories, she writes: "Catherine will choose. I offer more than she can use. Whatever is too close or too distant is ignored. If she wants to talk to the green robe, she may work with Winnicott's or Chodorow's texts. Or she may stick to Plato or Dewey or try Norman O. Brown" (44). These typewritten responses stand in between the student's narrative and the world of Grumet's childhood memories. They do not tamper with the integrity of the narratives. Students must decide what they will subject to further interpretation. These responses point to a world they can share: the arena of cultural experience. In this world, the wish to hide must be accommodated, but it is also a world where the wish to communicate can make use of the narratives, the curriculum, the classroom dialogue, and the teacher's love for the world to begin the work of fashioning stories that can make good their lives as teachers. The elements of surprise and curiosity, foreclosed by the French lesson but traced by Bloom in her work with Olivia, are anticipated in Grumet's pedagogy, where autobiographical narratives serve, not to reveal the world but to launch the possibility of finding things that matter and to sustain an appetite for the difficult work of teaching and learning with others and alone. In these last examples, the personal resists the stark opposition between public and private and between the individual and the social, but these apparent boundaries are not simply collapsed. Where the story of the French lesson focuses on the qualities of the personal that elude communication, Bloom and Grumet draw our attention to the ways in which we use the personal to make and renegotiate boundaries between our selves and the world.

If education can tolerate the play of hide and seek within the personal, the question is not whether or not we use the personal as a category for making knowledge in education. Instead, we might ask what we use the personal to do, how we account for its value, and what we choose to take up and ignore as we reflect upon our own and others' stories. The three times of the personal that so preoccupied Winnicott—illusionment, disillusion and re-illusionment—warn against placing too great a demand on the personal. At the same time, however, these dynamics of the personal help us to perceive difference, not merely as an obstacle to communication, but as a property that we create in fantasy and find in our encounters with the world. When we think of the personal as a method for working in the transitional space where inner and outer reality can be experienced together, we can begin to distinguish between these two kinds of reality.

Chapter Six

The Dreamwork of Autobiography: Felman, Freud, and Lacan

Psychoanalytic theory orients the question of women reading male theory toward a question of desire: what do women want from male theory?[1] I approach this question as traumatic by tracing the historicity of psychoanalytic reading practices through autobiography, a genre that offers epistemological force to feminist theory though not in predictable ways. The outline of my argument takes place neither fully anchored in the time of theory nor in the time of feminist politics but rather in a time that is other to both: dream time. Through the problem of dream interpretation, I consider debates on the nature of accepting psychoanalytic knowledge, a joke used by Freud, and theories of the subject derived through the writings of Jacques Lacan and Sigmund Freud but reconceptualized and renewed through feminist psychoanalysis. In the confrontation between psychoanalytic and feminist reading practices, Shoshana Felman is exemplary in holding the two in productive and creative tension, thus providing what I consider to be a valuable method for reconsidering feminist education even as feminist education also reconsiders the constraints and possibilities of education for women and girls. In order to take feminist and psychoanalytic reading practices together, we must take a detour through Freud and Lacan where, in a dream, we first encounter the unconscious. The singularity of dreams may be that these two apparently incompatible kinds of readings, feminist and psychoanalytic, can get tangled in each other rather than cancelling each other out.

Autobiography of a Reading Practice

> Of him all I have left is the fountain pen. I took it one day from my mother's purse, where she kept it along with some other souvenirs of my father. It is a kind of pen no longer made, the kind you have to fill with ink. I used it all through school. It "failed" me before I could bring myself to give it up. I still have it, patched with Scotch tape; it is right in front of me on my desk and makes me write, write.
>
> Maybe all my books have been the detours required to bring me to write about "that."
>
> —Sarah Kofman: *Rue Ordener, Rue Labat*

So begins Sarah Kofman's (1996) slim autobiographical volume. The translator describes the narrative as "an account of [Kofman's] childhood between the ages of eight and about eighteen: it begins on the last day she ever saw her father, 16 July, 1942—the day the Vichy police picked up Rabbi Bereck Kofman in the family apartment on the Rue Ordener—and ends when she enrolled at the Sorbonne in the midfifties" (vii). The translator, it seems, would like readers to know that Kofman's autobiography is about trauma, but Kofman's writing points to something more—the marking of the mark of trauma.

Kofman's "account" begins with the description of the fountain pen, and the significance of this beginning is not peripheral to her autobiography. The pen may no longer write, but its presence on the desk and the absence it marks "makes" Kofman write. And yet writing itself is posed as an extended detour away from her autobiographical writing. Her final sentence, ending with "that," points toward a quality of traumatic experience: it is unspeakable, "unclaimed" (Caruth 1996), an opaque kind of experience. Something happens, but the significance of the event arrives, if at all, belatedly. Traumatic experience creates a tear in our very capacity to make sense of the event, indeed, to fully experience the event. At the same time, we are drawn to the hole, compelled by some force to worry at it.

Kofman's writing about "that" has been deferred, but this deferral exceeds a simple putting off, just as its content also exceeds the painful event of the theft and murder of her father. In Freud's view, traumatic events can only be approached by means of deferred revision, what he calls *Nachträglichkeit.* The knitting up of the tear is a reconstructive project rather than, as much feminist work prefers, one of recovery and expression of unspeakable truth. The opening of Kofman's next-to-last work, one of several brief publications that focus on her personal history of loss and love during the Nazi occupation of France, asks us to consider two dynamics of this strange time of deferred action: the press onward (to write, to write) and the press of avoidance (the detours).

The interminable undulating force of *Nachträglichkeit* lies at the center of this chapter. I consider its movements in three overlapping contexts, each of which invites speculations for feminist educational theory. First, I discuss the centrality of the concept to psychoanalytic life-history making as a project of noticing how we find and lose sight of our capacity to apprehend what matters most to us: the surprise of intersection between our movements onward and our detours back. This first context suggests a method for reading feminist education and our own biographies as women and feminists in ways that do not settle what shall count as success and what as failure. My second context explores how Freud's own constant self-revision is read by Lacan in ways that allow psychoanalysis to be considered in radically new ways. Here the emphasis is on Lacan's observations about *Nachträglichkeit*, and the central place this term occupies in Lacan's reading of the psychoanalytic subject (Laplanche & Pontalis 1973; Laplanche 1999). This context serves as a reminder that feminist psychoanalysis that takes its cue from Lacan must consider his ties to Freud. Lacan "discovers" a psychoanalysis capable of holding in abeyance the satisfaction of mastery, whether mastery takes the form of application or critical opposition. Somewhat obliquely, this context is also animated by my growing worry that we feminists are in danger of forgetting how to use the rich legacy of feminist thought in favor of more contemporary contributions. A third context brings the project of *nachträglich* reading practices into conversation with the specificity of feminist readings of psychoanalysis. I turn to Felman (1993), as she revisits Freud's famous question, *What does a woman want?*, as well as some "canonical" feminist texts. Each context allows for a different articulation of the question that informs this edited volume. Following Adam Phillips' (1998) suggestion that psychoanalytic interpretations work best as hints to think with rather than orders to accept or reject, this chapter invites speculation on what might be useful here for the autobiographical project of feminist education.

Felman (1993), like Kofman, grapples with what it means to read and write autobiographically from a place marked by traumatic experience—in this case, the traumatic experience of being a woman living in a patriarchal culture. Her beginning premise, "that *none of us, as women, has as yet, precisely, an autobiography*" (14, emphasis in the original), seems counterintuitive given the rich bounty of women's autobiographies, the extensive feminist scholarship on the genre, and the tremendous pleasure many of us experience when we read women's autobiographies.

Felman's approach to women's autobiography also resonates with Kofman's observation that her philosophical and theoretical texts have served as the detours leading back to—making possible—autobiography. Felman generalizes this observation when she argues that women's autobiography must pass through the detours of literature and theory. Moreover, literature and theory must pass through the detours of autobiography. But Felman's essays are not autobiographical in any traditional sense: they do not narrate a life history. They narrate the autobiography of a reading practice.[2] What distinguishes this from other reading practices is the reconstructive tracing of self-implication: the force, significance, and surprise of *Nachträglichkeit*. However, because it is the woman who reads, Felman ties reading practices to sexual difference.

By bringing questions of sexual difference to the fore in relation to reading, writing, and autobiography, Felman extends her interest in the pedagogical lessons of psychoanalytic theory, bringing these into conversation with the pedagogical lessons of feminism. She offers us a new way to think about the historical tensions between psychoanalysis and feminism, performing thus what we can learn from Lacan while also suggesting something about the limits of that lesson. She brings her psychoanalytic insights about learning to bear upon her own biography as a female reader of texts written by men and those written by women. Like Lacan, and, indeed, *after* Lacan, Felman returns to the texts of Freud.

In a crucial way, the lesson Felman asks us to consider concerns Freud's (1919a) observation that learning *from* psychoanalysis is something quite different from learning *about* psychoanalysis. She sets this lesson in tension with what it means to learn *from* feminism in a way that is distinct from learning about feminism. In *Jacques Lacan and the Adventure of Insight*, Felman asks how "Lacan's unusual style and his unusual practice as a teacher…which makes a pedagogical imperative of its own refusal to take itself (its own authority) for granted, may suggest a revolutionary psychoanalytic lesson about lessons" (13). This lesson is revolutionary because it requires us to pay attention to qualities of pedagogical relations that interfere with (feminist) education's dream of progress and its corresponding reverence for linear, predictable development in terms of both the learner and knowledge. The dynamics of transference, the construction of and demands addressed to the illusory and idealized *subject-supposed-to-know*, and the persistence of our passion for ignorance (which often masquerades as a demand for knowledge) all point to the libidinal qualities of making and engaging knowledge that comprise the possibilities and constraints of education (Britzman 1998).

As we shall see, however, her rereading differs in important ways from Lacan's rereading. We might say that it takes up an insistence, articulated by both Lacan and Freud in their theoretical arguments, that the desire for mastery or for a master of the truth necessarily obscures and defends against knowledge of one's unconscious desire. Her reading of Freud relies on Lacan's for its method but not its substantive argument. Felman's argument is informed by the additional and deeply personal concern with how psychoanalysis *addresses* women. The lesson about reading across difference that Felman articulates performs a Lacanian lesson, but it can also be read as a lesson about reading Lacan. If, as Judith Feher Gurewich argues, "Lacan 'exists' only when read in dialectical relation with the Freudian text" (1999, viii), we might add that Lacan exists for feminists only when read in dialectical relation with feminist interpretations of the Freudian text, interpretations to which Lacan paid little attention.

Juliet Mitchell's *Psycho-Analysis and Feminism: Freud, Reich, Laing and Women* (1975) is often cited as the cornerstone for this modern feminist consideration of psychoanalysis. No doubt her well-established feminist Marxist credentials piqued feminist curiosity in her reclamation of Freud for feminism. While Lacan does not figure centrally in this project of reclamation, Mitchell points to his influence on a group of French Marxist feminists working under the name of *Psychoanalyse et Politique* to rethink what psychoanalysis offers to theories of social and political life. This group explicitly, though critically, brought psychoanalytic concepts to bear on their attempts to understand how ideology functions at the level of the subject.[3]

Felman navigates between feminist rejections of psychoanalysis and Juliet Mitchell's (1975) insistence that Freud's work offers an important analysis of patriarchy, not an endorsement of it. Felman is sympathetic to and respectful of the intellectual rigor of Mitchell's pioneering efforts to intervene in a dominant tradition within contemporary feminist discourse to discount Freud and reject psychoanalytic theory *tout court*. Still, she worries that Mitchell's approach may be too hasty in its implicit assumption that, because Freud was a great genius, he is "thus by definition innocent of any feminist critique" (1993, 69). She proposes a third way: "I would like to propose an approach that would take into account both what we can learn... from psychoanalysis about femininity and what we can learn from the feminist critique about psychoanalysis, in a way that would transcend the reified polarization of these two (as yet unfinished) lessons" (72). Felman distinguishes her approach to reading from Judith Fetterly's well-known feminist insistence that women become "resisting readers" as a way "to begin the process of exorcizing the male mind that has been implanted in us" (Fetterly, cited in Felman 1993, 5). While Felman admits that the project of exorcizing the male mind with which we have learned to read is attractive and necessary, her apprenticeship in psychoanalytic theory has taught her to be leery of approaches to reading that privilege counter-hegemonic consciousness. There is a danger, she argues, of failing to notice the difference between being a resisting reader and *resisting reading*. Slyly referring to the irksome conservatism of the ego, she notes that "resisting reading for the sake of holding on to our ideologies and preconceptions (*be they chauvinist or feminist*) is what we tend to do in any case" (6, emphasis added).

Nor does Felman rely on that other well-known, and increasingly contentious notion that we bring our embodied femininity to our reading (and writing) practices. Reading, for Felman, as for Lacan, is a psychical event. In this feminist story of reading, neither ideological consciousness nor biological femaleness can account for what happens when we read—or when our resistance to reading drops its guard—because neither coincides with the entirety of our reading selves. What cannot be accounted for in these approaches is the force of unconscious knowledge, what was earlier called *Nachträglichkeit.* This is, of course, one of Freud's most important discoveries. It is inconceivable, Felman observes, that Freud himself could be immune to the force of his discovery. Indeed, his discovery introduces a new and persistent epistemological problem; Felman notes that "psychoanalysis precisely teaches us that every human knowledge has its own unconscious, and that every human search is blinded by some systematic oversights of which it is not aware. This is true of psychoanalysis itself, which cannot exempt itself from its own teaching. And, of course, it is also true of feminism" (1993, 71). Felman reminds us that Freud considered his own theories of femininity to be provisional and that psychoanalysis itself represents a struggle to open up new questions or familiar questions in new ways. Freud's famous question *What does a woman want?* comes on the heels of his claim to have spent thirty years investigating "the feminine soul." This question has been a flash point for many feminist critiques of Freud. Felman, however, points out that even posing this question is unprecedented in the history of ideas. It acknowledges perhaps for the first time that masculinity and femininity cannot be known by appealing to anatomy. More than this, Felman suggests that Freud "puts in question…woman's *want* as the unresolved problem of psychoanalysis and, by implication, as the unresolved problem of patriarchy, telling us, again, that we *do not know* what a woman really wants" (73, emphasis in original).

Felman is less interested in the answers Freud tentatively formulates and revises over those thirty years than she is in the crisis of the question itself and how it forced itself on Freud. This orientation is the hallmark of the autobiography of reading practices. How, she wonders, did Freud live the question and live out its crisis? How Freud's autobiography passes through theory and how his theory passes through his autobiography form the intersecting storylines that Felman explores when she turns her attention to the dream that launched Freud's theory of dream interpretation. In a preamble to what has become known as "the dream of Irma's injection," Freud admits to his mixed feelings about his treatment, early on in his own development, of a family friend, Irma, whose hysterical symptoms had only been partially alleviated by his efforts. Prior to Irma's departure for the family's summer home, Freud had proposed a solution to the young woman that she seemed unwilling to accept. His dream is sparked by an encounter between Freud and a junior colleague who had been staying with the family. Freud heard a reproach in this doctor's news that the patient was "better, but not quite well" (1900/1901, IV, 106).

The dream features a party hosted by the Freuds. Irma was in attendance and complained to Freud about pains in her throat, stomach, and abdomen. At first, Irma was reluctant to let Freud examine her, but he succeeded in looking into her throat to discover "extensive whitish grey scabs upon some remarkable curly structures" (107). Three other doctors joined in the examination, which pointed to an infection that Freud blamed upon the use of a dirty syringe by the friend whom Freud thought was reproaching his methods of treatment. After recounting the events leading up to the dream and the dream itself, Freud provides a detailed analysis of his associations with the images as a demonstration of his method of dream interpretation.

Felman (1993) describes the significance of the dream in slightly different terms as she accounts for her interest in it. "I turn to this dream," she writes, "which, in yielding thus a key to dreams, in triggering Freud's greatest insight into dream interpretation, can be said to be the very dream from which psychoanalysis proceeds, because it is also a dream about femininity, and about Freud's relationship—professional and personal—to femininity. It is thus the singular confession of a singular male dream of singular theoretical and pragmatic consequences. *Perhaps it is significant that the relationship of Freud to women is precisely questioned in, and is the focus of, the very crisis dream from which psychoanalysis proceeds*" (74, emphasis added).

Autobiographical (dreamed by Freud), theoretical (interpreted by Freud), and literary (written by Freud) modes of giving expression to lived experience intersect here, but none fully exhausts nor fully accounts for the others. Indeed, these three modes of experience resist each other, and each embodies the resistance of the other. The time of *Nachträglichkeit*, then, is the time of self-difference and self-resistance.

As Felman charts her course through the details of the text of the dream and the text of Freud's interpretation of it, she also explores other interpretations of Freud's dream of Irma's injection, including several by feminist readers whom she reproaches for missing the insight of Freud's text in their rush to reveal its blindnesses. Lacan's reading of the same dream plays a minor role among the interpretations Felman examines. While, it is impossible to explore either of these rich interpretations in detail, a close look at the *differences* between what each claims the significance of the dream to be for psychoanalytic theory contributes to a contemporary consideration of creative, perhaps procreative, dialogue between psychoanalysis and feminism.

Dreamwork as a Joke

Lacan's (1991) discussion of the dream appears in Book II of *The Seminar of Jacques Lacan: The Ego in Freud's Theory and in the Technique of Psychoanalysis, 1954-1955.*[4] Like Felman, Lacan is interested in the crisis the dream provokes for Freud. His introductory comments refer to how his approach differs from those who argue that the dream of Irma's injection be interpreted as representing "a stage in the development of Freud's ego" (148). Lacan's notion of the significance of the dream is integral to the theory of the subject he develops over his career, a theory that rejects the developmentalism of ego psychology. For Lacan, the dream and its interpretation represent a stage in Freud's theory, not his ego. The pressures of onward movement and its detours are very much in evidence in Lacan's formulation of Freud's discoveries.

Lacan puzzles over Freud's claim to have discovered that the dream is always the fulfilment of a wish. In this dream, Freud identifies the wish to be absolved from responsibility for Irma's ongoing suffering. He absolves himself in several ways: Irma refuses his interpretation and thus has only herself to blame; Irma's pains were, after all, organic in nature, thus beyond his purview; Irma's suffering was directly related to her widowhood, something for which Freud was not responsible; Irma's pains were the result of an injection with a contaminated syringe administered by someone else. This rush of alternative explanations, each on its own exculpating Freud, reminds the dreamer of a joke:

> The whole plea—for the dream was nothing else—reminded one vividly of the defence put forward by the man charged by one of his neighbours with having given him back a borrowed kettle in a damaged condition. The defendant asserted first, that he had given it back undamaged; secondly, that the kettle had a hole in it when he borrowed it; and thirdly, that he had never borrowed a kettle from his neighbour at all. So much the better: if only a single one of these three lines of defence were to be accepted as valid, the man would have to be acquitted (Freud 1900/1901, IV, 119).

Freud's ironic observations point directly to the problem in structuring a defense on such conflicting claims: they cancel each other out, leaving the hapless accused once again without defense. In Felman's interpretation, this effect is a crucial performance of the unconscious, where "there is no such thing as an 'either-or', only a simultaneous juxtaposition" (1993, 93). On this point we can begin to tease out the differences between her reading and Lacan's. Lacan, in his retelling, poses the following question: "[H]ow is it that Freud, who later on will develop the function of unconscious desire, is here content, for the first step in his demonstration, to present a dream which is entirely explained by the satisfaction of a desire which one cannot but call preconscious, and even entirely conscious?" (1991, 151).

Lacan's response points to a problem that will preoccupy his theory of the subject. In that seminar, he insists that what is important to know is "where the subject of the analytic relation is to be found" (134). This puzzling assertion is, in turn, anticipated by Freud in a footnote that was added in 1919, nearly twenty years after *The Interpretation of Dreams* made its first appearance. This footnote is key, not only in relation to the development of Freud's second typology, but also to Lacan's rereading of Freud. It signals a correspondence between Freud's own return to the text and the question Lacan poses. The crux of the footnote reads,

> No doubt a wish-fulfilment must bring pleasure; but the question then arises "To whom?" To the person who has the wish, of course. But as we know, a dreamer's relation to his wishes is a quite peculiar one. He repudiates them and censors them—he has no liking for them, in short. So that their fulfilment will give him no pleasure, but just the opposite; and experience shows that this opposite appears in the form of anxiety, a fact that still has to be explained. Thus a dreamer in his relation to his dream-wishes can only be compared to an amalgamation of two separate people who are linked by some common element. Instead of enlarging on this, I will remind you of a familiar fairy tale....(1900/1901, V, 581)

The appearance of two separate people and the bond of anxiety that connects them is what interests Lacan. The footnote, insists Lacan, "expresses clearly the idea of a decentring of the subject" (1991, 135). He will go on to show us how the dream performs this decentered subject, the discovery of which, in theoretical terms, is alluded to in the footnote. The decentered subject is bound up with what Lacan calls "the sexual foundation" (137) which, he argues, in this dream is double. Its doubleness concerns the force of the collision between the dream's two primary qualities: it is a dream that Freud dreams as he tries to make sense of dreams, and it is a dream that concerns Freud's relations with the women in his life—notably his wife, pregnant at the time with Anna Freud, and a friend of Irma's, who strikes Freud as potentially less resistant to his help—who emerge in Freud's associations as he interprets the dream. This notion of the sexual foundation as double, then, refers to self-difference and difference between men and women.

There is something more at stake, and Lacan gives us a hint when he suggests that what Freud is trying to express in this complex dream is the idea that "[w]hat there is in the unconscious can only be reconstructed" (137). Not only does Freud "reconstruct" the significance of the dream with the addition of the footnote, but, in Lacan's view, the unconscious speaks indirectly, forcing its thinker to *interpret* its meaning. Three difficult and interconnected ideas are thus introduced in Lacan's interpretation. First, there is the idea of the (anxious) decentered subject found in the footnote that radically alters Freud's understanding of where wish fulfilment and pleasure occur in dreams. Second, we learn that this is a subject that is somehow bound up with sexual relations. In Lacan's view this signals the limits of possibility for relation rather than the grounds for closing the gap between or within individuals. Third, this subject reconstructs rather than discovers or recovers its otherness to itself. This last idea runs counter to the notion that the unconscious serves as container for repressed memories and represents the qualities of *Nachträglichkeit*, thereby distinguishing Lacan's contribution to this aspect of psychoanalytic theory.

Lacan proposes that this dream teaches Freud about the unconscious, a lesson that will eventually take on sharper meaning in Freud's postulation of the death drive and his second formulation of the psyche in terms of id, ego, and super-ego. Lacan finds the expression of the dream's lesson in the gap between Freud's speech in the dream and Freud's speech about his dream or, for that matter, about the emerging theories that will become psychoanalysis: "So this dream teaches us the following—what is at stake in the function of the dream is beyond the *ego*, what in the subject is of the subject and not of the subject, that is the unconscious" (1991, 159). How do we get a glimpse of this "beyond" that Freud cannot quite articulate? Lacan does not leave the "three feminine characters" (157) represented by Irma. These characters and the meanings associated with them are knotted together in the dream and form what Freud calls the "navel" of the dream, the knot of the unknown that resists interpretation. In the dream, Freud attempts to examine Irma and is surprised when she is, at first, reluctant to let him peer into her mouth. When she does open her mouth, he sees "on the right a large white spot and somewhere else…some remarkable curled structures which evidently are patterned on the nasal turbinal bones, extensive white-grey scabs" (1900/1901 IV, 107). Lacan considers what this "horrendous discovery" (1991, 155) signifies, noting,

> The phenomenology of the dream of Irma's injection led us to distinguish two parts. The first part leads to the apparition of the terrifying anxiety-provoking image, to

> this real Medusa's head, to the revelation of this something which properly speaking is unnameable, the back of the throat, the complex, unlocatable form...the abyss of the feminine organ from which all life emerges, this gulf of the mouth, in which everything is swallowed up, and no less the image of death in which everything comes to its end. (163–4)

Freud associates what he sees with the idea of death, linking it with both the grave illness of one of his daughters and a patient's death for which he felt professionally responsible. But Lacan takes this much further in his own remarkable set of associations. In a manner reminiscent of Melanie Klein's descriptions of the early phantasmatic and terrifying images the infant attributes to the mother, Lacan links the confrontation with the back of the throat to female genitalia and to death. What happens next, in the "second part" of the dream? In Lacan's words, "Freud appeals to the consensus of his fellow-beings, of his equals, of his colleagues, of his superiors" (1991, 164).

The two parts of the dream, then, are populated by two distinct casts of characters, the feminine characters who force Freud to the abyss of the unknown and unknowable, for which death is the ultimate representative, and a trio of male characters. If Freud confronts the knot of feminine resistance (and meets up with death or lack of being), he does so from the position of one whose *identifications* are bound up in a different knot—a cluster of male authority figures who play a key role in the dream and behind whom lurk significant characters from Freud's present and his childhood. It is the male characters who "play a ridiculous game of passing the buck with regard to these fundamental questions for Freud—*What is the meaning of the neurosis? What is the meaning of the cure? How well-founded is my therapy for neurosis?*" (Lacan 1991, 157, emphasis in the original).

The male characters do not provide Freud with the solution he wants. In the face of the contradictory answers produced by these characters who represent the sum of identifications of Freud's ego, Lacan argues that "the subject decomposes, fades away, dissociates into its various egos" (176). It is this failure of the ego to maintain its coherence that Lacan links to the subject's quest for signification set into motion by a terrifying encounter with the real. In the dream of Irma's injection, Freud confronts the lack of being, the other side of symbolization. A *different* Freud comes through this loss—this is the Freud who, in order to create psychoanalysis, hears his own questions and pursues them, in spite of uncertainty and disapproval. Lacan concludes by arguing that what is at stake in the dream is the very nature of the symbolic. "What gives this dream its veritable unconscious value, whatever its primordial and infantile echoes, is the quest for the word, the direct confrontation with the secret reality of the dream." He continues,

> In the midst of all his colleagues...of those who know—for if no one is right, everyone is right, a law which is simultaneously paradoxical and reassuring—in the midst of all this chaos, in this original moment when his doctrine is born into the world, the meaning of the dream is revealed to Freud—that there is no other word of the dream than the very nature of the symbolic (1991, 160).

Colette Soler (1996) helps us to situate Lacan's discovery of Freud's discovery at the beginning of Lacan's efforts to distinguish between the ego—that is, the sum of identifications—and the subject which comes into being and indeed must be made to appear through speech. *Speech* becomes a problematic term because it functions as mediation in the field of the ego and as revelation in the field of the subject. The mediating function of speech orients the ego in an address to another who can understand, maybe love, the one who speaks. For Lacan, Freud's dream performs such an address to his male colleagues and to the male authority figures behind them.

For speech to function as revelation, something happens that is completely new and unforeseen; revelation transforms the ego. In an encounter between two subjects, it is the singularity of the one who speaks that is made to appear. Again, to return to the dream, the singularity of Freud's desire—to conceive the answer to his questions—emerges in the rather strange space between Freud who dreams and Freud who returns to the dream in the footnote. When that which appears can be symbolized, it no longer resides "beyond the ego."

Lacan's project was to provoke, within the analytic setting, the paradox of assuming the position of a subject of desire. The subject comes into being when he or she can "become his or her own cause (...) come to be as subject in the place of cause. The foreign cause—that Other desire that brought him or her into the world—is internalized, in a sense, taken responsibility for, assumed...subjectified, made one's own" (Fink 1996, 89). In order for analysis to succeed—to be analysis—one must come to tolerate the disjunction between being and identification" (Soler 1996, 41), to learn how to put oneself in the place of the cause of one's own desire, and to partake in the interminable struggle to symbolize the cause of desire. Not only is this project interminable, but it also takes place in the strange time of *Nachträglichkeit*. The productivity of this version of subjectivity and its implications for theorizing all manner of relations within teaching and learning have yet to be fully realized. When considering the geography of such an undertaking, however, the differences between Lacan's reading and Felman's reading permit another way of conceptualizing the sexual foundation of Freud's discovery.

What Does Freud Want? Resistance and Sexual Difference

Felman also stresses the difference between Freud's dream speech and his speech about the dream, and she wonders about the function of the analogy between Freud's dream exculpations and the joke of the kettle. However, Felman, unlike Lacan, does not assume to be addressed by the joke. On this she agrees with other feminist readings of the dream. Why, she asks, have feminists been unable to detect Freud's insight that his wish fulfilment has the status of joke? She argues that this oversight has to do with the ways in which the joke, which connects Irma's resistance to the examination to her plea that Freud relieve her pain, comprises an exchange among men that refers, awkwardly and anxiously, to their relations to women. To women, Felman argues, the ridiculous game of passing the buck is just not funny.

However justified missing the joke may be, this response also misses the humor of the gap that the dreamed joke produces *for* the dreamer. "What is funny," Felman suggests, "in the joke...is that it refuses to resolve the question of the difference in terms of the logic of identity" (1993, 97). The wish fulfilment may be a joke, but the joke also performs anxiety. Where Lacan's interpretation separates the dream into two parts, one representing Freud's anxiety about his relations with women and his relation with death and a second representing "the sum of identifications" which make his ego, Felman brings these two parts in tension with each other and argues that the wish fulfilment functions as "a *denial* of the (sexual) anxiety of difference and self-difference." The kettle story is "first and foremost a *defense* against the conflict (crisis, contradiction, and self-contradiction) which provokes, and is embodied by, the dream" (97, emphasis in the original).

In order to trace the contours of the conflict that is embodied by the dream, Felman turns to the knot of female characters, focusing on Irma and Freud's wife. Where other interpreters of the dream focus on either the patient or the wife, Felman insists that it may be much more productive to consider the dreamwork in terms of "a *structural perception* of the symbolic *interaction* between the two" (103–4; emphasis in the original). In the dream Irma complains of pains in the abdomen but resists examination. In a footnote, Freud tells us that the pains remind him of his wife and his perception of her bashfulness towards him. Felman offers the observation that "[s]ince, out of the footnote, the wife emerges as a *secret sharer in the feminine complaint* of the hysteria, the feminine complaint as such unfolds as more complex than it first seemed, in that it now appears to be articulated from different vantage points, from different structural positions" (105, emphasis in the original). Felman considers the similarities and differences between the two female figures. Both demonstrate resistance toward Freud. Both have been "'infiltrated' by a male intervention" (105): Irma has had an injection from a dirty syringe, and Freud's wife has been impregnated. However, where Irma's complaint is traced back to her lack of a husband, the wife's complaint leads directly to the presence of a husband who considers himself happily married. How then can Freud's wife's complaint be accounted for when she represents the embodiment of female fertility? Felman argues that Freud stumbled upon the paradox that both women are "*suffering from the womb*" (106, emphasis in the original).

What does it mean that both women, who represent opposite poles of the criteria for fulfilment under patriarchal law, are unhappy? Felman's response to this is reminiscent of Lacan's insistence that the dream's wish speaks from beyond the ego, but she specifies how this "beyond" speaks as well from beyond "conventional ideas of feminine fulfilment" (106): "Notwithstanding Freud's own consciousness and cultural beliefs, the dream suggests that the patriarchal myth of feminine fulfilment *could be* but a masculine wish fulfilment" (106, emphasis in the original). Where there should be a difference between the positions each woman occupies, the dream renders them equivalent in their unhappiness. What the dream teaches Freud, in Felman's view, is that "the woman in his bed is as unknown, perhaps, and as dissatisfied, as the untalkative patient in his office, hysterically, and painfully choking on a speech she cannot yield" (107). In coming up against the question, What does a woman want?, another question appears: What does the dreaming Freud want? Most interpretations seem to agree that what he wanted was to *conceive* psychoanalysis by means of a homoerotic bond with his friend and colleague, Wilhelm Fliess.

Felman is not fully satisfied that the metaphor of conception is exhausted by these interpretations. She argues that it is significant that Freud does not simply wish to eliminate feminine resistance, but that "he wants to *understand* it, so that he can *answer* appropriately, relieve the suffering. Freud's fundamental wish is to *satisfy* each of these women: to satisfy the female wish" (107, emphasis in the original). If the dream's wish is to satisfy the female wish, how does the dream fulfill the wish? Two Freudian concepts, inversion and condensation, help Felman argue that the condensation of the two women into one and the inversion of what each gives Freud are the processes that permit Freud's dream to function as a wish fulfilment. We have returned to the time of *Nachträglichkeit*, a time that is neither representation nor identity but difference and self-difference. Freud's wife carries his child but refuses to address her husband with her desire. Irma, on the other hand, does address Freud with her complaint; she, however, refuses to make use of his therapeutic reply. Freud, Felman suggests, wants to conceive psychoanalysis with Irma who, unlike Fliess, offers Freud something that will prove key to psychoanalysis: Irma gives Freud her resistance. The significance of the dream for Felman concerns the radical alteration in the patient/doctor relationship. As Felman sees it,

> What emerges in the Irma dream as absolutely crucial is the recognition that fecundity—psychoanalytic fecundity—is *not conceptual*: the patient has to "*accept* the solution," that is, not just to integrate, but to participate in the conception of the insight. The doctor is no longer *master*—of the cure or of the patient, of the illness or of the "solution" to the illness. The analytical fecundity proceeds, precisely, from the doctor's destitution from his mastery...from the *destitution*, in effect, of mastery as such. (111, emphasis in the original)

This reading of what makes psychoanalysis an event that proceeds from transformed power relations between (male) doctors and their (female) patients resonates with Lacan's own understanding of the psychoanalytic dialogue. However, Felman traces the origins of the idea that psychoanalytic dialogue describes an exchange between "doctor and patient [who] are both self-divided, and [who] communicate through their self-division" (111) to the specimen dream that inaugurates psychoanalysis as a theory and as a method of self-analysis. Unlike Lacan, who locates the surprise of self-division beyond the sum of the ego's identifications with other male figures who represent the law, Felman locates the source of the discovery in Freud's identification with his female patient who represents unspeakable suffering:

> The doctor is creative (procreative) only insofar as he is himself a patient: Irma's symptom in the shoulder is Freud's own. The subject of the dream is saying: I am myself a patient, a hysteric; I am myself creative only insofar as I can find a locus of fecundity in my suffering. And I am procreative only insofar as I am not the master of that which I conceive, to the extent that I do not control what I give birth to. (111)

Felman has noticed something that Lacan has not. She pinpoints the risk of identifying with the one who does not represent the law, the one whose status as a speaking subject of desire is not yet assured. Her observation brings her to the conclusion, about Freud's creation, that

> [T]he dreamer is predicting here...that femininity—the question of woman and the woman as a question—is bound to remain unsolved and unresolved in psychoanalytic theory to the extent, precisely, that it is the very navel of psychoanalysis: a nodal point of significant resistance in the text of the ongoing dream of psychoanalytic dream of understanding. (120)

The dreamer's prediction is not of the same order as Freud's waking struggles as he continues to ask and be dissatisfied with his own responses to his question,"What does a woman want?" Felman points out that where the dream performs the wish to eliminate the conflict, the rhetorical structure of the question is one that addresses men exclusively. It is curious about women but does not speak to women. The impasse of waking relations for both men and women is the desire to be understood by the other as if difference made no difference. Lacan has helped us to theorize this desire for understanding as a trap of the ego, but it is an alluring trap nonetheless, both for psychoanalytic theory and for the participants who play by its rules. Indeed, it is the wish to be understood, as a woman, by her male analyst that has prompted Felman to write this essay on Freud. However caring and compassionate as a listener and astute as an observer Felman found this man to be, something was missing:

> Yet I felt that he might well have failed to understand, or to take into account, something crucial about me as a woman, thus someone in a different position than himself. I also felt that he had no warning of this something he was missing, since neither psychoanalytic theory nor his clinical training had prepared him for it, even though they enabled him effectively to understand me in other ways. (123)

Felman's wish to be understood as a woman by a man is structured like the plea of the hysteric who addresses her question about what it means to be a woman precisely to the one who cannot give her what she wants and then lets him know that she is not, will not be satisfied. The plea is addressed to an imagined Master, who must, as Freud learned and forgot many times, refuse the position. Or, as Gurewich writes, "By breaking down the collusion between the hysteric and her master, psychoanalysis allows the subject to sever the tie with the one who is by definition impotent to provide an answer to an impossible question" (1999, vii). This formulation, which teaches us a great deal about the nature of desire, emerges from reading Lacan who painstakingly traced Freud's steps as he repeatedly stumbled and regained his footing in his encounters with feminine resistance—that is, the resistance of his patients and his own self-resistance.

Eventually, using developments in Freud's theories as his base, Lacan would elaborate a theory of four discourses—those of the hysteric, the master, the university, and, finally, the analyst—to describe the forms social bonds take in the interminable struggle towards acceptance of the human condition: "To lack the answer becomes the solution. Beyond the mysterious power of the master and the opacity of knowledge there is nothing to be found except the freedom of desire" (Gurewich 1999, viii). If Freud's famous question was, What does a woman want?, Lacan's famous pronouncement would be, "La femme n'existe pas."

And perhaps she does not, at least not quite in the way much feminist writing has wished. Nor does the assertion exceed the structure of Freud's question to address women. Felman, even after writing her chapter on Freud, in an effort to give her analyst some clue about what he might be missing, still did not know how the chapter was also a testimony to her own autobiography as missing: missing because, she writes, "I still could not essentially address it to myself—truly address it, that is, to a woman" (1993, 124).

She leaves the question, What does a woman want? and moves to another scene of stories. This is the scene of women's struggles to address our stories, not (only) to a male audience, but to ourselves, to each other, to our mothers, and, most surprisingly, to our self-difference. Felman seems to have arrived, belatedly and through many detours, at her own implication in men's stories and to theories about women's desire.

A different question, one whose provenance Felman traces to the poetry of Adrienne Rich, situates women in relation to this other scene of writing: "with whom," Felman asks, "do you believe your lot is cast?" (1993, 126-27). This question, which relies on interpretation rather than ontology, is inclusive in its structure of address and can account for that other time, the dream life of desire. Because claiming this question as one of and for women's autobiography can only be a destination arrived at via a confrontation with the tensions of desire and that which resists desire, in short, via the detours of *Nachträglichkeit*, it returns us to the problem of education, of how knowledge comes to matter in belated time. Psychoanalytic theory, it is clear from all the kettle jokes, does not know what women want. Can we say that feminist education repeats this defense? When feminist education forecloses the question of resistance and forgets the problems of interpretation and self-implication, it may also be left with only a kettle story as a defense. However, the press onward and the detours backward that mark so creatively the autobiographies of Freud, Felman, and Kofman propose an alternative to kettle stories that resides in the question, How am I reading my life?

Notes

1. In choosing to pursue this question, I do not comment upon what Lacan has to say about masculinity and femininity and the psychical conflicts specific to each construct (See Mitchell and Rose 1982; Verhaeghe 1999). Rather, I explore Felman's (Lacanian) method for what it offers contemporary feminism as a way to read Lacan. The question is indebted to Elizabeth Young-Bruehl (1998).

2. The phrase "autobiography of a reading practice" deliberately invokes Jane Miller's (1996) "autobiography of a question" while also recognizing her emphasis on material conditions that organize the possibility of intellectual work.

3. It is less clear that Lacan's rereading of Freud has had much influence in feminist educational studies. This is particularly so if we think of educational studies in traditional ways, that is, as being primarily focused on teaching and learning in compulsory education. In this context, a sustained feminist study of Lacan has yet to make an appearance. Yet, the blossoming of an interest in pedagogy on the part of academics working in postsecondary humanities education (Berman 1994; Gallop 1995b; Penley 1989) has been accompanied by a re-opening of a space for thinking about the implications of psychoanalysis for educational research (Appel 1999, 1996; Briton 1997; Britzman 1998; Ellsworth 1997; Robertson 1997) that are 'post-Lacanian'. Felman has been central to both sites of this development.

4. Readers of French gained access to this seminar in 1978, but English-speaking readers had to wait an additional decade. These delays, which are justified by the enormity of the task of transcribing oral text and compounded by the ordinary difficulties of translation and the specific difficulties of translating Lacan's notoriously complex and playful language, contribute to the peculiar experience many of us have in attempting to read Lacan. Indeed, it is probably not unusual to have read commentaries long before encountering the material upon which they are based. There is a temptation, then, of giving an overly high regard to interpretations that meet our unexamined expectations and to forget that Lacan's ideas, much like those of Freud, changed, often significantly so, over time. My own focus on a very early Lacan and my discussion of only one other feminist reading of Lacan represent my interest in doing something with Lacan that might arouse curiosity rather than in explicating his teaching or failing in my own fashion to explicate his teaching.

Chapter Seven

The Use of the Teacher: Part I and Part II

This chapter brings together two conference papers I had originally hoped to make into one longer essay. At the 1997 meeting of the Conference on Curriculum Theorizing and Classroom Practice, I presented the first half under the title "Notes on Space and Curiosity: Winnicott on Learning." An earlier version of this paper, "The Use of the Teacher," was presented at the meeting of the Canadian Critical Pedagogy Association, also in 1997. In 1998, at this same conference, I revived the original title, calling my presentation "The Use of the Teacher, Part II." Both papers consider breakdowns in meaning. However, where my early work stayed close to the breakdowns in student meaning-making, particularly, in relation to demands of the curriculum, these essays consider a more dynamic understanding of resistance with an interest in exploring breakdowns between teachers and students and the different understandings each participant holds about the nature and significance of the conflict. Perhaps this enlarged world view can be partly accounted for by the fact that my own institutional role had changed from that of a student to that of a full-time faculty member with graduate and undergraduate teaching responsibilities. Returning to these essays, I am now surprised by the way they foreshadow the questions of implication I discussed in the first chapter.

My attempt to wrench the two short pieces into some coherent whole was oddly successful: "Hide and Seek: The Play of the Personal in Education" (Chapter Five) emerged from the effort. After writing the introductory chapter for this book, the relationship between Part I and Part II of the "The Use of the Teacher" has become clearer to me. Each begins with the assumption that there is much to be learned from studying breakdowns in meaning. Both parts focus on narratives of conflict between teachers and students that arise from the unruliness of erotic passions. The conflict is unleashed by different approaches to feminist teaching, both of which elaborate an understanding of the teacher as passionate and embodied and an understanding of pedagogy as collaborative meaning-making. In the first part, the metaphor for the teacher's embodiment is the maternal figure; in the second part, the teacher's passion for teaching is expressed in more overtly sexual terms. The conflicts erupting in both narratives suggest that we have returned to the knot Freud was up against when he tried to think about education and psychoanalysis together. Recall his failed attempt to articulate the possibility of mediating between the necessary taming of the instincts and their excessive repression. Part I and Part II tell two different stories about the insoluble knot at the center of teaching and learning and of teacher/student relations. The narratives at the center of these short essays remind us that our pedagogical efforts set into motion experiences the outcomes of which we cannot predict and often enough do not want. By writing and writing about such narratives, we come closer to seeing just how precisely they articulate what eros makes *inarticulate* in the work of teaching and learning. I have been calling these experiences breakdowns in meaning. It might be more appropriate to refer to them as experiences where meaning breaks apart, rendering visible, however briefly, the knot at the core of education and psychoanalysis. Let us now turn to the essays themselves. The two parts have been slightly revised and can be read in either order.

Part I

My early work with the implications of psychoanalysis for education focused on issues and qualities of students' resistance to knowledge. These are times when meanings break down, make no sense, or bother the learner's expectations. Mostly I was preoccupied with the question of how psychoanalytic notions of resistance help us make sense of how people learn and, more importantly, do not learn. As I was learning from doing this work, I began to understand that resistance is much more than an attitude or a stance that requires explanation—though this helps. I am now more curious about the ways in which resistance to knowledge moves as a dynamic, and, as such, requires the participation of more than one. I have picked up some clues about the implications of playing around with psychoanalytic theories of resistance for myself as an educator, friend, reader and scholar. In Chapter One, I explore my learning about and from educational and psychoanalytic theories. Chapters Two and Three consider some student narratives through the lens of questions of fantasy and resistance. The subsequent three chapters constitute a departure from an emphasis on resistance and focus more on narratives of creativity and the production of new ways of thinking. In this chapter I return to resistance as it sticks to teachers as well as to students. From this vantage, resistance becomes interesting, not merely as a category for thinking about the qualities of an individual's response to knowledge but also as a way of thinking through pedagogical relations that work across the time of learning and the time of teaching.

When we take resistance as the beginning rather than the explanatory end of analysis and when we study it as a dynamic, some of the conceptualizations offered by psychoanalytic object relations theorists become useful. This is so because object relations focus on the formation of the self through its relations with significant others. I want to look more closely at some of the concepts developed by Winnicott, beginning with his astonishing claim that there is no such thing as a baby. He expresses this notion repeatedly in his work, but here is a version that appears in a footnote to an essay written in 1960. He writes, "I once said: 'There is no such thing as an infant', meaning, of course, that whenever one finds an infant, one finds maternal care, and without maternal care there would be no infant" (1965, 39). Where this idea gets interesting for educators is here: for Winnicott, the breakdowns of meaning that occur between two subjects are necessary for the development of the individual. Let us take a closer look at the moves that Winnicott elaborates as he considers the work of the mother to facilitate the development of the human infant.

An infant begins life in a state of profound helplessness and becomes, if all goes well, a being who makes meaning out of life's chances and life's givens. Winnicott gathers these moves, developed throughout the body of his work, under the general rubric of the "good enough mother." He suggests that learning or development requires the capacity of the mother to manage in very ordinary and yet profound ways to be of use to the infant. As my title suggests, I am interested in exploring the parallels between the use of the mother and the use of the teacher.

Before turning to Winnicott, however, I am going to examine a story of a breakdown in pedagogical relations. This story takes us through a series of turns in understanding resistance in learning. The first turn asks us to consider the complications of making feminist classrooms when male students are present. When it was first published, the story was told from the perspective of the feminist teacher who locates resistance in the student. The story is retold about ten years later at a time when the stakes of feminist teaching are being rethought. This retelling, offered by Jane Gallop, locates resistance in the teacher and her pedagogical theory. In effect, the teacher refuses to be used by her male student. Gallop's retelling acts as a bridge for exploring the possibility of rethinking both poles of resistance, that is, where resistance is found either solely in the student or solely in the teacher. Following a discussion of Winnicott, we return to the story of the "not good enough" teacher and consider it in light of a teacher's capacity to tolerate being used by students.

The teacher's own biography, like that of the student, is made both inside and outside the institution. And, as Jane Gallop reminds us in "The Teacher's Breasts" (1995b) not only is that biography gendered—we might add sexed and raced as well—but what is deemed "personal" in the biographical can disrupt as well as enhance learning. Gallop attributes an interest in what is personal about teaching and learning to feminism, writing, "If the adjective 'personal' elevated to substantive status, has become a central focus for pedagogical theory, it is singularly due to the thinking and working of something called 'feminist teaching'" (79). In this essay, Gallop achieves several things that are salient to my meditation on the play between two categories: resistance and the personal. First of all, she offers a critique of the collapse between the feminine personal and maternal personal which has been so central to discussions of feminist classrooms. Second, she asks us to consider the ways in which, when it comes to those other scenes in the classroom, the personal cannot be reduced to a set of sociological attributes that determine the quality and qualities of pedagogical relations. Nor can it be reduced to facts and stories about one's life.

Gallop rereads Helene Keyssar's contribution to Margo Culley and Catherine Portuges' edited 1985 collection, *Gendered Subjects: The Dynamics of Feminist Teaching*. In familiar Gallopian style, she mines Keyssar's essay, titled "Staging the Feminist Classroom," for the tensions inherent in a model of pedagogy informed, explicitly or implicitly, by the early work of Nancy Chodorow. Gallop explains, "The teacher/student relation is again and again understood through analogy with the mother/daughter relation" (80). The central idea is a pedagogy based on nurturance, but the nurturance that is imagined turns out to be quite particular or, we might say, conditional. Furthermore, while nurturance is posed as being in opposition to authority, the turns of authority are very much at issue here.

Keyssar explores what happened in her mixed gender feminist classroom as students studied and acted out the scenes from a play chosen by the students themselves. I'll let Gallop sum up the script:

> The script they chose is Susan Miller's "Cross Country," a play with a classic seventies feminist protagonist who leaves her marriage for a more risky and fulfilling autonomy. This particular feminist heroine, named Perry, not only leaves her husband but also, in the same self-liberating gesture, leaves her job as a college teacher. The simultaneity of these two gestures suggests that, like marriage, teaching constrains women. (82)

Part of what Perry liberates herself from is the responsibility of grading the students' final papers. In the script, a male student is chosen to represent the class on this issue. When he meets with her in her office, not only does she remain adamant about not grading the papers but also kisses the student as she demands that he leave her office. The scene closes with the following stage directions: "He goes. But not without first touching her breasts" (83). In Keyssar's essay, relations between the actual (male) student and the (female) teacher break down when the acting male student, in his attempt to follow these directions, uses both hands to grab the breasts of the female student playing the part of Perry.

Gallop's reading of this event and the feminist teacher's interpretation of it emphasize the limits of imagining the erotics of teaching and learning as having nothing to do with sex. We have seen, in my discussion of Roger Simon's essay from the same edited collection, that talk of eros in teaching and learning can return as anxiety. However, Gallop also offers something quite troubling about the category of the "personal," particularly as it takes shape as an explanatory category that grounds learning and experience. As Gallop explores this story of classroom dynamics, where the desire to discipline and the desire to nurture collide with gendered bodies and gendered roles, it becomes clear that we cannot think of the "personal" as something that we possess. Rather, the personal emerges as a dynamic that is made in performance and remade within the work of interpretation. Resistance plays a role here. Keyssar constructs the male student as refusing to behave like a proper student. When she and the female students in the class try to correct his transgression, he resists these attempts as well. In Gallop's view, the surprise, for everyone involved, seems to be that he insists upon acting like a man, when what is required is for him to act like a student, here gendered female.

The story of resistance that Gallop tells is quite different from the one told by Keyssar. She writes, "Keyssar's interpretation tends toward embodying difference in the male student" (87). This, she goes on to explain, demonstrates an appropriation of Chodorow's model of gender in which "individuation is itself gendered male" (87). In this model, mother/daughter identification is pre-social and invaded by the masculinist world of the social. Those occupying a male body not only embody difference, they also introduce it, as interference, into the mother/daughter dyad. As Gallop suggests, a pedagogy modelled on this theory of development cannot tolerate difference, nor can it tolerate a notion of the erotic as sexual.

This key form of resistance—the resistance to difference—can be found in further symptoms that Gallop discovers in her meticulous attention to the text. First is the resistance to interpretation: the feminist teacher insists that the stage directions are unambiguous, that they require no interpretation.

While the events themselves call this into question, the male students, relying on narratives of seduction, and the female teacher and students, who rely on narratives of sexual harassment and gendered power relations, enact their gendered structures of power/knowledge/erotics.

Second, Keyssar's own non-interpretive interpretation relies upon a misreading. She offers the following as the proper approach to the stage directions: "The young man would no more grab her breasts and caress them than he would disfigure a painting in a museum. He might, however, fleetingly touch a painting—or a breast—to test its reality and to determine limits" (Keyssar, cited in Gallop, 87). Grab, caress, disfigure; breasts, painting in a museum; breasts, breast. Gallop has a lot of fun with the cacophony of images here, and her attention to the slippage between breasts, as erotic symbol, and a breast as a symbol of maternal nurturance seems very astute to me.

Let us return to the two key concepts upon which her discussion relies. These are "difference" and "interpretation." Even if these categories are symptomatic of the limits of a pedagogical model informed by the particular readings of Chodorow's early appropriations of psychoanalytic theory that dominated feminist classrooms in the late seventies and eighties, it might still be the case that object relations theory offers a productive way of thinking about an eros particular to pedagogical relations, the dynamics of learning/not learning, and the work of teaching. Rather than return to Chodorow, I want to explore the pre-feminist, but post-Freudian work of Winnicott because his writing offers some interesting conceptualizations of space and time that might allow us insight into that other scene of teaching: the capacity of the teacher to be used. I am going to focus primarily on the work of teaching, but I must note that, when it comes to Winnicott and object relations, one must begin with the mother or with the work of mothering. Generally speaking, object relations theory has appealed to feminists precisely because of its focus on mother/child relations and its emphasis on the primacy of object-love over pleasure-seeking. Winnicott, who is one of the most important figures of this school of psychoanalytic theory, has also been subject to feminist critique. Claire Kahane (1992) summarizes the feminist complaint:

> Winnicott's formulations...are deeply problematic, not only in their focus on the mother as the origin of the self and their lack of attention to maternal ambivalence and aggressivity, but in their exclusion of the cultural context of meaning in which the mother and infant move, a symbolic network structured along the axis of the masculine subject which holds them both. What is the effect of language on the

> maternal mirror? How do internalized cultural codes influence maternal perception of the infant and vice versa? (287)

Kahane's discussion, while offering a useful cautionary note, also raises some new difficulties. These cannot be resolved here, but, in my view, her emphasis on cultural context threatens to lose sight of the psychical nature of development that Winnicott theorizes. More than this, and contrary to Kahane, my reading of Winnicott convinces me that he pays exquisite attention to maternal ambivalence and aggressivity. It is precisely these features that have drawn me to his work. Perhaps a friendlier commentator can help me set the stage a bit differently by describing what distinguishes Winnicott's object relations theory from classical Freudian theory. Adam Phillips offers insight into some of the difficulty of acknowledging the full significance of the mother:

> For Freud, in short, man was the ambivalent animal; for Winnicott, he would be the dependent animal....Prior to sexuality as the unacceptable, there would be helplessness. Dependence was the first thing, before good and evil. (1988, 7)

Now, ambivalence, defined as "the simultaneous existence of contradictory tendencies, attitudes or feelings in the relationship to a single object" (Laplanche & Pontalis 1973, 26), is an extraordinarily useful concept (see Britzman 1998), and I am not advocating abandoning either it or Freud's theory of instincts that allows us to think about libidinality as pleasure-seeking. I will come back to ambivalence, reading it through the lens that Winnicott offers. From original and terrifying dependence but full of potential for developing into a human being, the infant that Winnicott considers proceeds gradually to realize where she begins and where the other leaves off, what she controls and what exceeds her grasp, and, most significantly, how to tolerate, indeed, take pleasure in experiences of both connectedness and separation and experiences in which understanding and mastery are delayed. None of this work can be done alone; the infant requires an other to accomplish—or begin to accomplish—these early tasks of learning. This is why Winnicott argued that there is no such thing as a baby. Rather, there are always two, and in this strange mathematics, two becomes three for the space between the two is where these questions become observed, delayed, engaged, and so on. Missed meaning, a theme taken up in Chapter One, and its recovery both belong to this space.

Before Winnicott became a psychoanalyst, he was a pediatrician. He spent countless hours observing mother/infant dyads in health and in distress. He brought his insights about the qualities of these relationships to bear upon his psychoanalytic practice and his learning from his practice. The scene of the mother/child and the scene of the analyst/analysand, in Winnicott's work, are analogous, and he works back and forth across both, allowing each to refine the other. Unlike Freud, apparently, Winnicott had few qualms about putting himself in the place of the mother. As we shall see, the work of the mother may be socially gendered, but it may not be as psychically gendered as feminist critics of psychoanalysis argue. Let us look more closely at the qualities of being that are facilitated by "good enough" self/other relations. While the contexts of creating a new individual out of a baby and of transforming the adult analysand can be thought together, the adult who enters analysis is not the same as the infant he or she once was; still, within psychoanalytic theory generally, there is an understanding that the organization of events and perceptions from early childhood do become elaborated as persistent psychic structures over the period of a lifetime. There is something quite accidental about how this occurs, and learning, both within and without the psychoanalytic dialogue, is possible because we can study how these structures repeat, work through new content, and become refined. When it comes to analogies, it seems to me that classroom dynamics might be more reminiscent of analysis than they are of the original scene.

Still, we begin with the baby. The infant comes into the world completely dependent upon the care of another, usually the mother. Good enough care refers to the qualities of attunement of the mother with her baby. Attunement moves back and forth, *potentially* exactly as required, from, on the one hand, providing the infant with the illusion of herself as omnipotent, thus containing the terrors of dependence, to, on the other hand, the gradual disillusionment of omnipotence that allows the infant to tolerate and exceed dependence, to recognize and enjoy the other, and to take pleasure in discovery. The "omnipotent" baby creates, as if by magic, the world. Only gradually does she come to experience it as always having been there. An unspoken pact exists between the mother and the baby: she does not ask the vulnerable infant, "Did you create that or did you find it?" I will discuss four concepts that Winnicott developed as he paid attention to the dynamics of learning, the movement between creation and discovery, within the psychoanalytic experience. I discuss them in the chronological order in which they emerge in Winnicott's life-long curiosity about how self-hood is constituted, lived, and reconstituted.

In much the same way that the fort-da game played by Freud's little grandson Ernst became an occasion for Freud's discovery of the death drive (1920), infants' use of a shiny spatula became a cornerstone of Winnicott's speculations about the dynamics of analysis (1992a). He would put the spatula within reach of an infant who was held quietly by his mother. He observed that the infant would invariably reach for the spatula but would hesitate before finally grasping it and using it as a plaything. The moment of hesitation was crucial, for it signalled to Winnicott an acceptance on the baby's part of the reality of his own desire. From there, Winnicott began to think of the analyst's interpretations as glittering objects offered to the analysand to do something with. What becomes important here is not the content of the interpretation, but whether and how it is used. The gift of the interpretation must be genuine; the analysand must be free to take it, leave it, pick it up at some other time, and even destroy it.

The hesitation that initiates purposeful activity also constitutes the seedling of a more elaborated notion—the capacity to be alone. The capacity to be alone describes a quiet relaxed state that also precedes creative work:

> The infant is able to become unintegrated, to flounder, to be in a state where there is no orientation, to be able to exist for a time without either being a reactor to an external impingement or an active person with a direction of interest or movement. (1992a, 34)

Rather than understanding silences in the analytic encounter as the frustrating symptoms of resistance on the analysand's part to forge on with the work of analysis, Winnicott observed that silence was frequently the evidence of the analysand's wish and capacity to be alone—with the analyst present. Just as the mother must be able to tolerate not knowing when her own wish to take up the baby or play with her will be felt as an intrusion into the baby's fledgling self-experience, so too must the analyst be able to withstand uncertainty about the meaning of a silent period and to adjust to a correction made by the analysand.

The third concept requires even more equanimity on the part of the mother or analyst. This concerns the capacity to allow for hate in the relationship. Winnicott was insistent that caregivers need to acknowledge and find ways of satisfying their natural and inevitable feelings of ambivalence towards their children. The child, according to Winnicott, needs hate—a term which he uses to catch everything from mild annoyances to murderous fantasies—in order to come to terms with her own aggression in a healthy way. For Winnicott, there can be no construction without destruction. Winnicott notes that some analysands wear the analyst out because they cannot relate to the analyst as a whole person with whom they can identify. Winnicott has a very creative way of managing his hate:

> (...) I have ways of expressing hate. It is expressed by the existence of the end of the hour. This is true even when there is no difficulty and the patient is pleased to go. (1992b, 197)

The final concept brings me to the title of this paper and to the final years of Winnicott's writing. It will also be the starting point for travelling backwards through the concepts just discussed in order to say something about their pedagogical implications. The concept is "the capacity to use the object." Winnicott distinguishes between object-relating and object-usage, and it is important to note that, in his developmental schema, object-usage comes later and constitutes the grounds for living life creatively. Here is how Winnicott defines object-relating:

> (...) the subject allows certain alterations in the self to take place of a kind that has caused us to invent the term cathexis. The object has become meaningful. Projection mechanisms and identifications have been operating, and the subject has been depleted to the extent that something of the subject is found in the object, though enriched by the feeling. (1971b, 88)

Finding an object meaningful still belongs to the realm of creating the world and its objects. It is, therefore, an important step in the elaboration of a self that can acknowledge the reality of desire. But this mode of self-fashioning is not yet sufficient. The work of creating objects is the work of a subject in isolation even though the objects that surround the subject are involved. A more fulsome practice of self-fashioning requires a move from creating objects to finding them already there. It is in this movement that a firmer boundary between the me and the not-me can be elaborated. This shift, which marks the beginning of object-usage, is characterized, on the one hand, by a recognition of the illusoriness of the qualities one has invested in the object (which is not the same thing as abandoning it altogether) and, on the other hand, by a recognition of the nature and behavior of the object that belongs to itself. Winnicott writes, "the object, if it is to be used, must necessarily be real in the sense of being part of shared reality, not a bundle of projections" (1971b, 88).

Where object-relating is an experience of the subject-in-isolation, object-usage is an experience of the subject in relation to other subjects:

> (...) usage cannot be described in terms of the individual subject...usage cannot be described except in terms of the object's independent existence, its property of having been there all the time. (1971b, 88)

The movement between object-relating and object-usage is never guaranteed. Like the hesitation that occurs between reaching for the shiny spatula and grabbing hold of it, something quite dramatic marks the space in between object-relating and object-usage:

> This thing that there is in between relating and use is the subject's placing of the object outside the area of the subject's omnipotent control; that is, the subject's perception of the object as an external phenomenon, not as a projective entity, in fact recognition of it as an entity in its own right. (89)

In essence the subject "destroys" the object as it exists for the subject. To put it somewhat differently, the subject must lose the object as it functions for the self alone in order to find it and use it for the purposes of shared world-making.

The work of other/object is crucial here: the object must survive and be perceived as surviving this assault in the moment of destruction. It is the survival, i.e., the non-retaliation, of the mother/analyst/teacher that allows the child/analysand/student to begin to tolerate and even enjoy living in a world where words do not mean what you want them to and where other people exist whose desires oppose your own (Castoriadis 1994, 6). What becomes possible is the co-existence of two contradictory feeling states: "I destroyed you. I love you."

Let us return to the story of Keyssar and her students. In that difficult scene, meaning breaks down when competing libidinal attachments are acted out in the process of bringing Miller's fictional script to life. Neither the male student nor the teacher seems willing to acknowledge that the fictional script is a representation of the messiness of the creative act of living, where construction and destruction co-exist and transformation is both desired and delayed. By refusing interpretation, both between the script and the world and between the classroom participants and the script, the teacher and her students lose the possibility of considering their own attachments to a reality that they might wish could be otherwise. Construction requires destruction, at least at the level of fantasy.

The male student and the feminist teacher, it seems to me, are both implicated in the prescriptive fantasies of world-creating, the world of object-relating. Neither seems to have the strategies for moving to a more ambiguous yet creative space of world-discovery, where the differences of the other can be used to enrich the self while also acknowledging the other's otherness. Perhaps, in these early moments of development of feminist classrooms, the illusory qualities of world-creating were exactly what everyone could tolerate. It may be the case that the time of the political and the time of the pedagogical are always, to borrow one of Freud's famous phrases, a phase apart. As I reflect upon my own practices of teaching and theorizing classroom dynamics, I find that I have become much more curious about the spaces in between my own "I destroyed you. I love you." Like Winnicott's end of the hour, there are ways I can express my hate: I leave the classroom, wear skirts that would lead to censure in a school, read a book that is too difficult for my students, talk to my colleagues, even write an essay....I have become more capable of withstanding my students' need to move from "I destroyed you to I love you," in the process of their becoming more invested in learning about the qualitative differences between creating objects in isolation and the more tentative work of discovering them in the space of classroom talk and work.

Part II

There is, as we have seen, something quite curious about teacher/student relations. For teachers and students alike, it is difficult to describe just what is going on in our classrooms. The drama of the curriculum, with its logic of inclusions and exclusions, surprises, and "difficult texts," may be relatively easy to pinpoint. The conflict discussed in Part I suggests another drama in the worries and hopes, the jealousies and friendships, and the wishes to be recognized or left alone that play themselves out in a circus of affect that no one seems to be in charge of. Legal and rational forms of institutional authority are no match for the unruly passions that flare up and disappear only to reappear in different guises.

I want to take a closer look at this relational chaos as it is described by Gallop in another text. The combustible teacher/student relations discussed in *Feminist Accused of Sexual Harassment* (1997) move to a more intimate set of circumstances. The essay discussed in the first section of this chapter centers on a textual reading, but this small volume describes a serious and protracted conflict between Gallop and some of her graduate students. When the book first appeared, it was eagerly read by students and faculty members in Education and Women's Studies graduate programs. Discussions of it in the hallways and classrooms where I work also tended to replicate the dynamics Gallop is talking about. Neither the chaos nor its tendency to repeat comes as any surprise to psychoanalysis and its curiosity about what goes on in the space of the analytic dialogue. I draw upon a few of the insights of two psychoanalytic theorists, Sigmund Freud and Jessica Benjamin, as I consider the analytic space of the classroom in relation to the particularities of Gallop's story.

One of the questions Gallop's text raises and tries to work through—with mixed success, I think—is a question that has been central to my work: what can education learn from studying the breakdowns in teacher/student relations? As we learned from Keyssar, these breakdowns frequently mean something to the teacher that is quite different from what they mean to the student. The "use of the teacher" becomes even more complicated in this narrative. How can these different meanings be ethically engaged and worked through by any two people, who, in addition to being complex idioms in their own right, are also positioned in particular ways by institutional structures of demands and responsibilities?

Jessica Benjamin's (1998) discussion of some developments in psychoanalytic theory helps us to see how this dilemma is reminiscent of some of the dilemmas facing Freud and the early patients he referred to as hysterics. Freud has been severely criticized for his apparent incapacity to see these women as anything more than a bundle of symptoms to be used to advance his theories of mind and human development. We must keep in mind, however, that many of Freud's patients, including some of those more severely disabled during their illnesses, went on to lead very productive lives. Many became psychoanalysts ready to debate Freud on his own stomping grounds. It is equally important to recall that theoretical breakthroughs emerged from the breakdowns in these early analytic relations. Indeed, as we shall see, contemporary psychoanalytic theorizing continues to benefit from reconsiderations of these case histories.

Benjamin offers a historical exploration of the parallels as well as the differences between two bids for freedom, feminism and psychoanalysis, that both relied upon and undermined Enlightenment ideals. One movement considers the costs of patriarchy; the other, the costs of civilization. They find a common figure in Bertha Pappenheim, also known as Anna O. Anna O. was the famous hysteric whose treatment with Freud's early collaborator, Joseph Breuer, was foundational to the development of psychoanalysis as the talking cure. Bertha Pappenheim founded the German Jewish women's movement and is considered to be a forerunner of modern social work. Benjamin suggests that it is useful to explore the identification with Anna O./Bertha Pappenheim because she incarnates for the first time and in a most compelling way that dual identity which each psychoanalyst-patient pair, separately and together, must embody. She writes:

> The contradictions of Anna/Bertha—which appear through the split image of the helpless, fragmented patient versus the articulate stalwart feminist who defends the helpless—reflect the split in every analyst, who is her/himself subject to as well as subject of the analytic process. (8)

Benjamin brings the disparate figures yet singular person of Anna O. and Bertha Pappenheim together in order to highlight the radical move on Freud's part to reject hypnosis for the more collaborative project of the talking cure, which enlists the active participation of the patient in the project of alleviating her suffering. Benjamin describes this move as the primary leap of psychoanalysis; however, as we are well aware, leaping about in the unknown is risky business. Benjamin argues that a serious dilemma presents itself when the analyst poses as the subject who already speaks, and the analysand is relegated to the position of the Other who does not yet speak for herself. In this early formulation, it might be more accurate to say that the symptom speaks through the patient, and the analyst's task is to unravel the secret code of the symptom and return its meaning to the analysand. As Benjamin and others remind us, this compromise formation was particularly disastrous in Freud's aborted and by all accounts mishandled encounter with another famous hysteric, Dora (1901/1905).

Dora did speak for herself and what she told Freud was, on the one hand, a love story: Dora was in love with and identified herself with Frau K. On the other hand, Dora told a sordid tale about her father's attempts to make a gift of her to Frau K's husband so that the father could himself enjoy the company of Frau K. On one level, Freud must have "heard" this story because it is his account of it that we have received. On another level, however, Freud remained adamant that Dora was not telling the truth about her desire. What could not yet be spoken in Freud's estimation was Dora's repressed wish to take her own mother's place as her father's love object.

Dora's story raises doubts about the inevitability of the smooth operations of the oedipal complex and the acquisition of gender identity. No less significantly it positions Freud, like Dora, as an odious, indeed feminized, object of exchange in Dora's father's selfish transactions. Indeed, Freud was startled to realize that he shared with Dora's governess the ignominy of having been dismissed with a fortnight's notice. In spite of his humiliation, Freud's reflections on the case convinced him to enlarge the arena of the patient's active role in helping herself. Her freedom from suffering must emerge from her willingness to identify with the analyst's authority, thus putting him, at least temporarily, in the place of her ego ideal. As Benjamin argues, this is a dangerous project as it is predicated upon exceeding the rational exercise of weighing the truth value of the analyst's authoritative interpretations and actually freeing the self from habitual conscious constraints in order to actively participate in the reenactment of unresolved conflicts in the analytic relationship. Still, the analyst must take care to keep his own objectivity intact. Freud compares the analyst's approach to the volatility of the transference to the chemist's work with dangerous chemicals. As Benjamin observes, however, the metaphor fails because the analyst is as much chemical as chemist insofar as s/he "is a force in the combustion of the transference" (17).

What Freud seems to have trouble meeting head on is the impossibility of maintaining objective detachment. Indeed, the analyst's specialized knowledge and investments in that knowledge can work against the shift between acting out desire and claiming desire. Referring again to Dora's failed analysis, Benjamin speculates:

> Freud's notion that the patient could identify with the ideal side of the analytic authority momentarily forgets the equally plausible reaction of rejecting authority: that the patient would also attack the analyst precisely because of [the analyst's] investment in the role of healer (against which Freud also warns) would call forth the hidden dimension of power in knowledge, which cannot win out against unreason without the usual consequences of subjugating a binary opposite. (21)

Benjamin responds to the impossibility of the analyst's neutrality by acknowledging the need to attend to the analyst's unconscious desires as these come to bear upon the analytic relationship. It has always been the case that the patient must learn to think twice about who she imagines she is speaking to and from what position she speaks. Benjamin suggests that such learning be reciprocal, that is, that the analyst, who is affected in the exchange, must also wonder about what shapes her own participation. This development may have important implications for thinking about education and knowledge production in academic settings.

The dilemmas of feminist education may be particularly instructive insofar as such education begins with the assumption that women, historically silenced, can and do speak about their experiences of being women in a society that may still not have gotten used to the idea. Even so, in institutional settings, such as the university classroom, feminists worry that the inherent inequalities between teachers and students may repeat rather than repair female students' social location as oppressed subjects. This pressing concern returns us to the figure of Anna O./Bertha Pappenheim and Benjamin's observations that the subject of psychoanalysis is one who moves back and forth between helplessness and autonomy and between not yet speaking for herself and speaking out on her own behalf. She represents not only the figure of woman (and Other) for psychoanalysis but also, in Benjamin's formulation, the analyst whose knowledge, investments, ambivalences, and unconscious wishes emerge precisely where the autonomy of another is at stake. She may also represent the feminist who speaks both *as* a woman and *on behalf of* women who speak but are not yet heard. She may, in fact, represent feminism itself which must tread precariously, arguing for women's equality using an equality that does not yet exist.

The risks, pleasures, and blind spots in teacher/student relations can be glimpsed in Gallop's discussion of the events culminating in charges of sexual harassment made against her by two women graduate students. One narrative line of the book traces Gallop's incredulity about what happened to her; a second and related narrative deals with the collisions between feminist perspectives on sex and power in the university. The second narrative poses the question of what sex has to do with learning. For Gallop, who relies upon her own biography as an undergraduate and graduate student in the early 1970s, the pleasures of sex, knowledge, and learning are inextricably linked, each enhancing and elaborating Gallop's experience of herself as in charge of herself, as a subject of desire. As we saw in Part I, Gallop is critical of feminist approaches to education that refuse the sexual dimensions of teaching and learning. For her accusers, sex, knowledge, and learning are also linked, but they emphasize how erotic attachments between teachers and students interfere with, rather than enhance, students' capacity to learn and to take pleasure in knowledge production.

Both parties lay claim to the wish to create conditions of possibility for female students in higher education. Both parties also ground their arguments in feminist politics and feminist knowledge about what women need in order to become subjects on their own terms. The split subject of Anna O. Bertha Pappenheim reappears here. The split, however, seems to be formulated somewhat differently—as the capacity and the absence of capacity to give consent. Gallop insists that the risks inherent in assuming that her students are already subjects of desire and fully capable of risking consent are both necessary and worthwhile. In its most extreme form, the sexual harassment policy assumes female students whose consent is the effect of traumatized femininity and, hence, impossible to give or take back. Gallop links this perspective, not only to the impossible project of rationalizing learning and teacher/student relations but also to the censorship of intellectual curiosity, knowledge production, and academic freedom.

In the first narrative, this split subject also reappears, this time in the intimate relations between the students and Gallop. Both students have been enamored of Gallop and all she represents, but both have also been disappointed by her response to their academic efforts. A difficult observation must be made: when it comes to psychic reality, the difference between justified and acceptable demands and those that are too harsh, mistaken, or debilitating cannot be determined in advance. These students withdraw their investments in identifying with Gallop as an ego ideal and instead identify her with a position of authority, which they resist. They express their resistance as follows: Gallop really wanted to have sex with them; they rejected her, and she retaliated. Gallop argues that her pedagogical investment in a blatantly sexualized teacher/student relationship can result in exciting and rewarding learning for everyone involved, but she also admits that this play is volatile and risky. Sometimes these relationships break down dramatically as seems to have been the case here. We need to consider what might be lost when the recognition sought from and perceived to be withheld by the teacher turns into the need to destroy the teacher, and this need is abetted by the institution.

The formulations of object relations theory discussed in Part I can help us here. Each student's position as subject is temporarily displaced when she moves to take up the position of object of the institution's authority. This authority perceives her as helpless in terms of her capacity to negotiate with Gallop.

A second loss concerns the capacity to tolerate the difference of another. Recall that Winnicott argues that it is a developmental achievement to learn to accept the nature and behavior of the other as belonging to itself and outside of the control of the self. It is a precarious achievement that is haunted by earlier fantasies that the other is magically created by the self with the sole purpose of narcissistic self-gratification. The fantasy can only be broken by another fantasy. In this second fantasy, the other who does not conform to the wishes of the self is attacked and destroyed. It is only by virtue of the survival of the other that the fantasy gives way to the capacity to tolerate the other on the other's own terms. For the students, once the formal complaint has been lodged, this fantasy can no longer play itself out within the relationship.

A third loss concerns the difficulty for Gallop herself to reflect upon her own limited tolerance to identify with the students once they cease to remind her of her former self. As a jubilant graduate student, Gallop may have been successful in her bid, at the level of fantasy, to "destroy" her smart professors by getting them naked. She insists that sex with her professors humanized them for her. These professors apparently survived her efforts to bring them to her level, and their professional relationship proceeded.

As Gallop tells the story, the two students began to believe that Gallop really wanted to have sex with them and that they were rejecting her when, at a graduate student gay and lesbian conference, Gallop tried to make a joke. In the context of formulating a question to one of the presenters, Gallop blurted out that graduate students were her sexual preference. Gallop tells us this story with the suggestion that she paid dearly for a bad joke. But a joke can only be "bad" if it does not tickle unconscious wishes and fears. This joke may have been too good, that is, on target, for the students and even Gallop to bear. In her public proclamation, Gallop reduced her bantering, sexually playful relationship with the two students to a category choice.

Ironically, this takes us back to Dora. In her discussion of Dora, Benjamin cites remarks made by Gallop in another context about Freud's incapacity to solve the mysteries of women's sexuality. Benjamin writes:

> If Freud (1905) thinks that he who disdains the key, which is sexuality, will never open the door to the patient's mind, then Dora, as Jane Gallop (1985) remarks, is there to let him know that no one wants to be opened with a skeleton key. (15)

Gallop's students, it seems, are also here to remind us that neither the teacher's biography nor the pedagogical imperatives that spring forth from it tell the whole story of the chaos and ambivalence of erotic relations in teaching and learning. Gallop's response, in *Feminist Accused of Sexual Harassment*, may also be a reminder of the limits of institutional remedies for breakdowns in teacher/student relations. Such remedies cannot be used to defer endlessly the more precarious and difficult work of trying to make sense of these breakdowns. In turn, something is revealed of the particularities of the "knots" at the center of our most beautiful and personal pedagogical dreams.

Bibliography

Abelove, Henry, Michèle Aina Barale & David Halpern, eds. *The Lesbian and Gay Studies Reader*. New York & London: Routledge, 1993.

Appel, Stephen. *Positioning Subjects: Psychoanalysis and Critical Educational Studies*. Westport, CT: Bergin & Garvey Press, 1996.

——, ed. *Psychoanalysis and Pedagogy*. Westport, CT: Bergin & Garvey Press, 1999.

Apple, Michael. "On Analyzing Hegemony," *Journal of Curriculum Theorizing* 1(1) (1979):10–27.

Bannerji, Himani, Linda Carty, Kari Dehli, Susan Heald & Kate McKenna. *Unsettling Relations: The University as a Site of Feminist Struggles*. Toronto: Women's Press, 1991.

Belenky, Mary, Blythe Clinchy, Nancy Goldberger & Jill Tarule. *Women's Ways of Knowing: The Development of Self, Voice, and Mind*. New York: Basic Books, 1986.

Benjamin, Jessica. *Like Subjects, Love Objects: Essays on Recognition and Sexual Difference*. New Haven & London: Yale University Press, 1995.

——. *Shadow of the Other: Intersubjectivity and Gender in Psychoanalysis*. New York & London: Routledge, 1998.

Berman, Jeffery. *Diaries to an English Professor: Pain and Growth in the Classroom*. Amherst: University of Massachusetts Press, 1994.

Bloom, Leslie. *Under the Sign of Hope: Feminist Methodology and Narrative Interpretation*. Albany, NY: State University of New York Press, 1998.

Bogdan, Deanne. *Re-educating the Imagination: Toward a Poetics, Politics and Pedagogy of Literary Engagement*. Portsmouth, NH: Boynton/Cook-Heinemann, 1992.

——. "When Is a Singing School (not) a Chorus? The Emancipatory Agenda in Feminist Pedagogy and Literature Education." In *The Education Feminist Reader*, edited by Linda Stone. New York: Routledge, 1994, 349–358.

Bollas, Christopher. *Hysteria*. London & New York: Routledge, 2000.

——. *Free Association*. Cambridge: Icon Books/Totem Books, 2002.

Borch-Jacobson, Mikkel. "The Oedipus Problem in Freud and Lacan." *Critical Inquiry* 20(2) (1994): 267–282.

Bowles, Gloria & Renate Klein, eds. *Theories of Women's Studies*. New York: Routledge, 1983.

Brennan, Teresa. "Introduction." In Teresa Brennan (ed.), *Between Feminism and Psychoanalysis*. London & New York: Routledge, 1989, 1–23.

Briskin, Linda & Rebecca Coulter. "Feminist Pedagogy: Challenging the Normative." *Canadian Journal of Education/Revue Canadienne de l'education* 17(3) (1992): 247–263.

Briton, Derek. "Learning the Subject of Desire." In Sharon Todd, ed., *Learning Desire: Perspectives on Pedagogy, Culture, and the Unsaid*. New York & London: Routledge, 1997, 45–72.

Britzman, Deborah. *Practice Makes Practice: A Critical Study of Learning to Teach*. Albany, NY: State University of New York Press, 1991.

—. "Structures of Feeling in Curriculum and Teaching," *Theory into Practice* 31(3) (1992): 252–258.

—. "Is There a Queer Pedagogy? Or Stop Reading Straight." *Educational Theory*, 45 (2) (1995a):151–165.

—. "The Question of Belief: Writing Poststructural Ethnography," *QSE: International Journal of Qualitative Studies in Education* 8(3) (1995b): 229–238.

—. "The Tangles of Implication," *QSE: International Journal of Qualitative Studies in Education* 10(1) (1997): 31–37.

—. *Lost Subjects, Contested Objects: Toward a Psychoanalytic Inquiry of Learning*. Albany, NY: State University of New York Press, 1998.

—. *After-Education: Anna Freud, Melanie Klein, and Psychoanalytic Histories of Learning*. Albany, NY: State University of New York Press, In Press.

— & Alice Pitt. "Pedagogy and Transference: Casting the Past of Learning into the Presence of Teaching." *Theory into Practice* 35(2) (1996):117–123.

Brodkey, Linda. *Academic Writing as Social Practice*. Philadelphia: Temple University Press, 1987.

Bunch, Charlotte & Sanda Pollack, eds. *Learning Our Way: Essays in Feminist Education*. Trumansberg, NY: The Crossing Press, 1983.

Butler, Judith. *Bodies That Matter: On the Discursive Limits of Sex*. New York: Routledge, 1993.

—. "Against Proper Objects," *differences: A Journal of Feminist Cultural Studies* 6 (3 & 4), (1994):1–26.

The Canadian Oxford Dictionary, Katherine Barber, ed. Toronto, Oxford & New York: Oxford University Press, 1998.

Caruth, Cathy. *Unclaimed Experience: Trauma, Narrative, and History*. Baltimore & London: Johns Hopkins University Press, 1996.

Castoriadis, Cornelius. "Psychoanalysis and Politics." In Sonu Shamdasani & Michael Münchow, eds., *Speculations After Freud: Psychoanalysis, Philosophy and Culture*. London & New York: Routledge, 1994, 1–12.

Chodorow, Nancy. *Power of Feelings: Personal Meaning in Psychoanalysis, Gender and Culture*. New Haven & London: Yale University Press, 1999.

Cochran-Smith, Marilyn. *Inside/Outside: Teacher Research and Knowledge*. New York: Teachers College Press, 1993.

Connelly, Michael & Jean Clandinin. *Teachers as Curriculum Planners: Narratives of Experience*. New York: Teachers College Press, 1988.

Convery, Andy. "Listening to Teachers' Stories: Are We Sitting Too Comfortably?" *QSE: International Journal of Qualitative Studies in Education* 12(2) (1999): 131–146.

Cornell, Drucilla. "Gender, Sex, and Equivalent Rights." In Judith Butler & Joan Wallach Scott, eds. *Feminists Theorize the Political*. New York: Routledge, 1992, 280–296.

Culley, Margo & Catherine Portuges, eds., *Gendered Subjects: The Dynamics of Feminist Teaching*. Boston: Routledge & Kegan Paul, 1985.

de Lauretis, Teresa. *Technologies of Gender: Essays on Theory, Film and Fiction*. Bloomington, IN: Indiana University Press, 1987.

Eigen, Michael. "The Psychotic Self." In *The Psychotic Core*. Northvale, NJ: Jason Aronson, 1986, 313–363.

Elbaz, Freema. *Teacher Thinking: A Study of Practical Knowledge.* London: Croom Helm, 1983.

Ellsworth, Elizabeth. "Why Doesn't This Feel Empowering? Working Through the Repressive Myths of Critical Pedagogy," *Harvard Educational Review* 59(3) (1989):297–324.

——. *Teaching Positions: Difference, Pedagogy, and the Power of Address.* New York: Teachers College Press, 1997.

Ernst, Sheila. "Gender and the Phantasy of Omnipotence: Case Study of an Organization." In Barry Richards, ed., *Crises of the Self: Further Essays on Psychoanalysis and Politics.* London: Free Association Books, 1989, 101–111.

Felman, Shoshana. *Jacques Lacan and the Adventure of Insight: Psychoanalysis in Contemporary Culture.* Cambridge, MA: Harvard University Press, 1987.

——. *What Does a Woman Want: Reading and Sexual Difference.* Baltimore, MA: Johns Hopkins University Press, 1993.

Fink, Bruce. "The Subject and the Other's Desire." In Richard Feldstein, Bruce Fink & Maire Jaanus, eds., *Reading Seminars I & II: Lacan's Return to Freud.* Albany, NY: State University of New York Press, 1996, 76–97.

Finke, Laurie. "Knowledge as Bait: Feminism, Voice, and the Pedagogical Unconscious," *College English* 55 (1993):7–27.

Fletcher, John. "Psychoanalysis and the Question of the Other." Introduction to *Essays on Otherness* by Jean Laplanche. London & New York: Routledge, 1999, 1–51.

Foucault, Michel. *The History of Sexuality, Volume One: An Introduction*, translated by Robert Hurley. New York: Vintage Books, 1980.

Freud, Anna. *Four Lectures on Psychoanalysis for Teachers and Parents.* 1930. *The Writings of Anna Freud.* Vol 1. New York: International Universities Press, 1974, 73–133.

Freud. Sigmund. In James Strachey, ed. and trans., *The Standard Edition of the Complete Psychological Works of Sigmund Freud.* In collaboration with Anna Freud. Assisted by Alix Strachey and Alan Tyson. 24 vols. London: Hogarth Press and The Institute of Psychoanalysis, 1953–1974.

——. *The Interpretation of Dreams*,1900–1901. *Standard Edition* IV & V.

——. "Some Reflection on Schoolboy Psychology," 1914. *Standard Edition* XIII, 241–244.

——. "On the Teaching of Psychoanalysis in Universities," 1919a [1918]. *Standard Edition* XVII, 169–173.

——. "The Uncanny," 1919b. *Standard Edition* XVII, 219–256.

——. "Beyond the Pleasure Principle,"1920. *Standard Edition* XVIII, 7–64.

——. "Two Encyclopaedia Articles," 1923a[1922]. *Standard Edition* XVIII, 235–259.

——. "The Ego and the Id," 1923b. *Standard Edition* XVIV, 3–59.

——. "Negation,"1925. *Standard Edition* XVIV, 235–239.

——. *New Introductory Lectures on Psycho-Analysis*, 1932. *Standard Edition* XXII, 7–182.

Fuss, Diana. *Essentially Speaking: Feminism, Nature, and Difference.* New York: Routledge, 1995.

Gallop, Jane. *Around 1981: Academic Feminist Literary Theory.* New York: Routledge, 1992.

——,ed. *Pedagogy: The Question of Impersonation.* Bloomington, IN: Indiana University Press, 1995a.

——. "The Teacher's Breasts." In Jane Gallop, ed., *Pedagogy: The Question of Impersonation*. Bloomington, IN: Indiana University Press, 1995b, 79–89.

——. *Feminist Accused of Sexual Harassment*. Durham & London: Duke University Press, 1997.

Giroux, Henry A. "Theories of Reproduction and Resistance in the New Sociology of Education: A Critical Review," *Harvard Educational Review* 53 (3) (1983): 257–293.

Grosz, Elizabeth. "Lesbian Fetishism?" *differences: A Journal of Feminist Cultural Critique* 5(2) (1991): 39–54.

Grumet, Madeleine. *Bitter Milk: Women and Teaching*. Amherst, MA: University of Massachusetts Press, 1988.

——. "The Beauty Full Curriculum," *Educational Theory*, 39(3) (1989): 225–230.

——. "Scholae Personae: Masks for Meaning." In Jane Gallop, ed., *Pedagogy: The Question of Impersonation*. Bloomington, IN: Indiana University Press, 1995, 36-45.

Gurewich, Judith Feher. Preface to *Does the Woman Exist? From Freud's Hysteric to Lacan's Feminine* by Paul Verhaeghe. Translated by Marc du Roy. New York: The Other Press, 1999, vii–ix.

Horney, Karen. *Self-Analysis*. New York: W. W. Norton, 1942.

Jacobus, Mary. *Psychoanalysis and the Scene of Reading*. Oxford: Oxford University Press, 1999.

Julien, Isaac. *Looking for Langston*. United Kingdom: Sankofa Film and Video. 1988.

Kahane, Claire. "Object-Relations Theory." In Elizabeth Wright, ed., *Feminism and Psychoanalysis: A Critical Dictionary*. Oxford: Basil Blackwell Ltd., 1992, 284–290.

King, Katie. "Lesbianism as Feminism's Magical Sign: Contests for Meaning and U.S. Women's Movements, 1968–1972." In *Theory in Its Feminist Travels: Conversations in U.S. Women's Movements*. Bloomington, IN: Indiana University Press, 1994, 124–137.

Knoblock, Peter & Arnold. P. Goldstein. *The Lonely Teacher*. Boston: Allyn & Bacon, 1971.

Kofman, Sarah. *Rue Ordener, Rue Labat*. Translated by Ann Smock. Lincoln & London: University of Nebraska Press, 1996.

Lacan, Jacques. "The Mirror Stage as Formative of the Function of the 'I' as Revealed in the Psychoanalytic Experience." In *Écrits: A Selection*, translated by Alan Sheridan. New York: Norton, 1977.

——. "The Difficulties of Regression;" "The Dream of Irma's Injection;" and "The Dream of Irma's Injection (conclusion)." In Jacques Alain Miller, ed., *The Seminar of Jacques Lacan, Book II: The Ego in Freud's Theory and in the Technique of Psychoanalysis, 1954–1955*. Translated by Sylvanna Tomaselli. New York & London: W. W. Norton & Co., 1991, 134–171.

——. *The Seminar of Jacques Lacan: On Feminine Sexuality: The Limits of Love and Knowledge. Book XX, Encore 1972–1973*. Translated with notes by Bruce Fink. New York & London: W.W. Norton & Co., 1998.

Ladson-Billings, Gloria. "Silences as Weapons: Challenges of a Black Professor Teaching White Students," in *Theory into Practice* 35(2) (1996): 79–85.

Laplanche, Jean. *New Foundations for Psychoanalysis*. Translated by David Macey. Cambridge: Basil Blackwell Ltd., 1989.

——. "Notes on Afterwardsness." In *Essays on Otherness*. London & New York: Routledge, 1999, 260–265.

—— & Jean-Bertrand Pontalis. *The Language of Psychoanalysis*. Translated by Donald Nicholson-Smith. New York: W. W. Norton, 1973.

Lather, Patti. *Getting Smart: Feminist Research and Pedagogy with/in the Postmodern*. New York: Routledge, 1991.

Lewis, Magda. "Interrupting Patriarchy: Politics, Resistance, and Transformation in the Feminist Classroom," *Harvard Educational Review* 60(4) (1990): 468–488.

Luke, Carmen & Jennifer Gore, eds. *Feminisms and Critical Pedagogy*. New York & London: Routledge, 1992.

Lusted, David "Why Pedagogy," *Screen*, 27(5) (1986): 2–14.

Maher, Frances & Mary Kay Thompson Tetreault. *The Feminist Classroom: An Inside Look at How Professors and Students Are Transforming Higher Education for a Diverse Society*. New York: Basic Books, 1994.

Martin, Biddy. "Sexualities Without Genders and Other Queer Utopias," *Critical Crossings*, 24 (2–3) (1994):104–121.

Martindale, Kathleen. "Theorizing Autobiography and Materialist Feminist Pedagogy," *Canadian Journal of Education/Revue Canadienne de l'education* 17(3) (1992): 321–340.

McCarthy, Cameron. *Race and Curriculum*. London: Falmer Press, 1990.

——& Warren Crichlow, eds. *Race, Identity and Representation in Education*. New York & London: Routledge, 1993.

McRobbie, Angela. *Feminism and Youth Culture: From Jackie to Just Seventeen*. Boston: Unwin Hyman, 1991.

Miller, Jane. *School for Women*. London: Virago Press, 1996.

Miller, Janet L. "Autobiography as a Queer Curriculum Practice." In William Pinar, ed., *Queer Theory in Education*. Mahwah, NJ & London: Lawrence Erlbaum, 1998, 365–373.

Millot, Catherine. *Freud, Anti-pedagogue*. Paris: Bibliotheque d'Ornicar. 1979.

Mitchell, Juliet. *Psycho-Analysis and Feminism: Freud, Reich, Laing and Women*. New York: Vintage Books, 1975.

—— & Jacqueline Rose. *Feminine Sexuality: Jacques Lacan and the École Freudienne*. London: Macmillan, 1982.

Munro, Petra. "Resisting 'Resistance': Stories Women Teachers Tell," *Journal of Curriculum Theorizing* 12(1) (1996):10–28.

Ottinger, Ulrike. *Bildnis Einer Trinkerin (Ticket of No Return)*. 1979.

Penley, Constance. "Teaching in Your Sleep: Feminism and Psychoanalysis." In *The Future of an Illusion: Film, Feminism, and Psychoanalysis*. Minneapolis: University of Minneapolis Press, 1989, 165–181.

Person, Ethel. *By Force of Fantasy: How We Make Our Lives*. New York: Penguin Books, 1995.

Phelan, Peggy. *Unmarked: The Politics of Performance*. New York: Routledge, 1993.

Phillips. Adam. *Winnicott*. Cambridge, MA: Harvard University Press, 1988.

——. *The Beast in the Nursery: On Curiosity and Other Appetites*. New York: Pantheon, 1998.

——. "The Pragmatics of Passion." In *Promises, Promises: Essays on Literature and Psychoanalysis*. London: Faber & Faber, 2000, 296–309.

Pinar, William & Madeleine R. Grumet. *Toward a Poor Curriculum*. Dubuque, IA: Kendall/Hunt, 1976.

—, William M. Reynolds, Patrick Slattery & Peter M. Taubman. *Understanding Curriculum*. New York: Peter Lang, 1995.

Pitt, Alice. *Subjects in Tension: Engaged Resistance in the Feminist Classroom*. Unpublished doctoral dissertation. University of Toronto, 1995.

—. "Reading Resistance Analytically: On Making the Self in Women's Studies." In Leslie G. Roman & Linda Eyre, eds., *Dangerous Territories: Struggles for Difference and Equality in Education*. New York & London: Routledge, 1997, 127–142.

— & Deborah Britzman. "Speculations on Qualities of Difficult Knowledge in Teaching and Learning: An Experiment in Psychoanalytic Research," *QSE: International Journal of Qualitative Studies in Education*, In Press.

Rich, Adrienne. "Compulsory Heterosexuality and Lesbian Existence," *Signs* 5 (1980): 631–660.

Riley, Denise. *Am I That Name? Feminism and the Category of 'Women' in History*. Minneapolis: University of Minnesota Press, 1988.

Robertson, Judith P. "Fantasy's Confines: Popular Culture and the Education of the Female Primary School Teacher," *The Canadian Journal of Education/Revue Canadienne de l'education* 22(2) (1997):123–143.

Rosenwald, George C. & Richard Ochberg. "Introduction: Life Stories, Cultural Politics and Self-Understanding." In George C. Rosenwald & Richard Ochberg, eds., *Storied Lives: The Cultural Politics of Self-Understanding*. New Haven: Yale University Press, 1992,1–18.

Schafer, Roy. *The Analytic Attitude*. New York: Basic Books, 1983.

—. *Retelling a Life: Narration and Dialogue in Psychoanalysis*. New York: Basic Books, 1992.

Scheurich, James. "A Postmodernist Critique of Research Interviewing," *QSE: Qualitative Studies in Education* 8(3) (1995): 239–253.

Scott, Joan. "Gender: A Useful Category of Historical Analysis," *American Historical* Review 91 (1986):1053–1075.

—. "Experience." In Judith Butler & Joan Scott, eds., *Feminists Theorize the Political*. New York: Routledge, 1992.

Sedgwick, Eve Kosofsky. *Epistemology of the Closet*. Berkeley, CA: University of California Press, 1990.

Sherman, Cindy. *Untitled Film Stills*. London: Jonathon Cape. 1990.

Silverman, Kaja. *The Subject of Semiotics*. New York: Oxford University Press, 1983.

—. *The Acoustic Mirror: The Female Voice in Psychoanalysis and Cinema*. Bloomington: Indiana University Press, 1988.

—. *Male Subjectivity at the Margins*. New York & London: Routledge, 1992.

—. *The Threshold of the Visible World*. New York: Routledge, 1996.

Simon, Roger. *Teaching Against the Grain: Texts for a Pedagogy of Possibility*. New York, Westport, CT: Bergin & Garvey, 1992.

—. "Face to Face with Alterity: Postmodern Jewish Identity and the Eros of Pedagogy." In Jane Gallop, ed., *Pedagogy: The Question of Impersonation*. Bloomington, IN: Indiana University Press, 1995, 90–105.

Sleeter, Christine. "How White Teachers Construct Race." In Cameron McCarthy & Warren Crichlow, eds., *Race, Identity and Representation in*. New York & London: Routledge, 1993, 157–171.

Soler, Colette. "The Symbolic Order (I & II)." In Richard Feldstein, Bruce Fink & Maire Jaanus, eds., *Reading Seminars I & II: Lacan's Return to Freud*. Albany, NY: State University of New York Press, 1996, 47–55.

Steiner, George. "On Difficulty." In *On Difficulty and Other Essays*. Oxford: Oxford University Press, 1980, 18–47.

Todd, Sharon. *The Pedagogical Imaginary and Trans/formation: Rethinking Teaching and Learning Beyond Identity*. Unpublished doctoral dissertation. Concordia University, Montreal, 1996.

—— ,ed. *Learning Desire: Perspectives on Pedagogy, Culture and the Unsaid*. New York & London: Routledge, 1997.

Verhaeghe, Paul. *Does the Woman Exist? From Freud's Hysteric to Lacan's Feminine*. Translated by Marc du Roy. New York: Other Press, 1999.

——. "Teaching and Psychoanalysis: A Necessary Impossibility." In *Beyond Gender: From Subject to Drive*. New York: The Other Press, 2001, 35–47.

Wallon, Henri. *Les origines du caractère chez l'enfant: les préludes du sentiment de personnalité*. Paris: Bovin et Cie, 1934.

Walters, Suzanne Danuta. "From Here to Queer: Radical Feminism, Postmodernism, and the Lesbian Menace (or, Why Can't a Woman Be More Like a Fag?)." *Signs* 21(4) (1996): 831–869.

Weiler, Kathleen. "Freire and a Feminist Pedagogy of Difference," *Harvard Educational Review* 15(2) (1991): 449–474.

——. "Remembering and Representing Life Choices: A Critical Perspective on Teachers' Oral History Narratives," *QSE: International Journal of Qualitative Studies in Education* 5(1) (1992): 51–62.

Weis, Lois. *Working Class Without Work: High School Students in a De-industrializing Economy*. New York: Routledge, 1990.

Willinsky, John. "Getting Personal and Practical with Personal Practical Knowledge," *Curriculum Inquiry* 19 (3) (1989): 247–264.

Willis, Paul. *Learning to Labour*. Lexington: Heath, 1977.

Winnicott, Donald Woods. "Communicating and Not Communicating Leading to a Study of Certain Opposites," 1963. In *The Maturational Processes and the Facilitating Environment: Studies in the Theory of Emotional Development*. Madison, CT: International Universities Press, 1965, 179–192.

——. *Playing and Reality*. London & New York, Routledge, 1971a.

——. "The Use of the Object and Relating Through Identifications," 1969. In *Playing and Reality*. London & New York: Routledge, 1971b, 86–94.

——. "The Capacity to Be Alone," 1958. In *Maturational Processes and the Facilitating Environment: Studies in the Theory of Emotional Development*. London: Hogarth Press and The Institute of Psycho-Analysis,1965. Reprinted London: Karnac Books, 1990, 29–36.

——. "The Observation of Infants in a Set Situation," 1941. In *Through Paediatrics to Psycho-Analysis: Collected Papers*. New York: Brunner/Mazel, 1992a, 52–69.

——. "Hate in the Countertransference," 1947. In *Through Paediatrics to Psycho-Analysis: Collected Papers*. New York: Brunner/Mazel, 1992b, 194–203.

——. "Transitional Objects and Transitional Phenomena," 1951. In *Through Paediatrics to Psycho-Analysis: Collected Papers*. New York: Brunner/Mazel, 1992c, 229–242.

Wittig, Monique. "The Straight Mind," *Feminist Issues* 1 (1) (1980): 105–111.

——. "One Is Not Born a Woman," *Feminist Issues* 2 (1) (1981): 47–54.

Young-Bruehl, Elisabeth. "On Psychoanalysis and Feminism." In *Subject to Biography: Psychoanalysis, Feminism, and Writing Women's Lives*. Cambridge, Massachusetts & London: Harvard University Press, 1998, 174–194.

Zeichner, Kenneth & Daniel Liston. *Teacher Education and the Social Conditions of Schooling*. New York: Routledge, 1991.

Zimmerman, Bonnie. "What Has Never Been: An Overview of Lesbian Feminist Literary Criticism." In Elaine Showalter, ed., *The New Feminist Criticism: Essays on Women, Literature and Theory*. New York: Pantheon Press, 1985, 200–224.

Index

-G-

-H-

-I-

-J-

-K-

-L-

-M-

-N-

-O-

-P-

-R-

-S-

-T-

-U-

-V-

-W-

Complicated Conversation

A BOOK SERIES OF CURRICULUM STUDIES

This series employs research completed in various disciplines to construct textbooks that will enable public school teachers to reoccupy a vacated public domain—not simply as "consumers" of knowledge, but as active participants in a "complicated conversation" that they themselves will lead. In drawing promiscuously but critically from various academic disciplines and from popular culture, this series will attempt to create a conceptual montage for the teacher who understands that positionality as aspiring to reconstruct a "public" space. *Complicated Conversation* works to resuscitate the progressive project—an educational project in which self-realization and democratization are inevitably intertwined; its task as the new century begins is nothing less than the intellectual formation of a public sphere in education.

The series editor is:

Dr. William F. Pinar
Department of Curriculum and Instruction
223 Peabody Hall
Louisiana State University
Baton Rouge, LA 70803-4728